Sarah Brown's
QUICK AND EASY
Vegetarian
COOKERY

Sarah Brown's
QUICK AND EASY
Vegetarian
COOKERY

BBC BOOKS

PHOTOGRAPHY *Monique Le Luhandre*
FOOD PREPARATION *Berit Vinegrad*
STYLING *Rebecca Gillies*
ILLUSTRATIONS *Hannah Firmin*

Published by BBC Books
A division of BBC Enterprises Ltd
Woodlands, 80 Wood Lane
London W12 0TT

First published 1989
Reprinted in 1989 (twice)
Reprinted in 1990 (three times)
Reprinted in 1991

ISBN 0 563 20695 0

Typeset in 10½/13pt Cheltenham Light and printed
and bound in England by Mackays of Chatham PLC
Colour origination by Technik Ltd, Berkhamsted
Colour printed by Lawrence Allen
Cover printed by Clays Ltd, St Ives PLC

CONTENTS

ACKNOWLEDGEMENTS

*T*his book has been fun to write, and when it came to testing recipes, thanks to the nature of the subject, extremely quick! I would like to thank Beverley Muir for her help with the cooking and inevitable washing-up; Kenwood for the loan of food processing equipment; Nina Shandloff for her help in initiating the project; Cath Speight for the design of the book; and Sarah Hoggett who painstakingly brought the final manuscript together.

As always, I have had tremendous support throughout from Harriet Cruickshank, and from Paul Street who, although he can't cook, is terrific at organising ideas and eating vast quantities of experimental recipes!

INTRODUCTION

*M*uch as I love planning, preparing and cooking recipes, there are many occasions when I am simply short of time and need to rustle up a meal in a hurry. I'm sure I am not alone. One of the main criticisms of vegetarian cookery is that it seems time-consuming and involves much forward planning. There's the image of beans soaking overnight and huge quantities of vegetables waiting to be scrubbed and chopped. But there are many techniques that will help you save time. It is not just a matter of having a recipe that cooks in a few minutes, but also looking at methods of preparation, how to avoid too much shopping, and making full use of kitchen gadgets.

For this reason, this book is not set out like a conventional cookery book, with recipes based on similar types of ingredients – pasta, grains and pulses, eggs, cheese, vegetables and so on – grouped together. Instead, each chapter focuses on one aspect of saving time, and contains tips to help you devise your own quick meals as well as specific recipes. With the exception of the two chapters which cover quick starters and puddings, the recipes are generally for main courses.

Store-cupboard Ingredients deals with quick-cooking wholefood ingredients such as rice, lentils and tofu, which you should certainly keep in stock. Mainly Vegetables deals with dishes in which the main ingredients are vegetables. Although vegetables sometimes take a little longer to prepare, they are generally quick to cook.

One-pot Recipes concentrates on sauces and casseroles. This type of meal is both simple to prepare and economical on washing-up! This chapter also has notes on using a pressure cooker, as this is the most appropriate time-saving gadget to use with these types of recipes. Time-saving Gadgets deals with using other equipment that can speed the cooking or preparation in some way and includes notes on the different types of machines available.

Simple Salads deals with raw food – a sure-fire way of saving on cooking time! There are tips on how to turn salads into proper meals and notes on quickly made dressings.

Livening-up the Leftovers gives you some basic recipes such as an all-in-one sauce and a quick crumble topping, plus tips on using leftovers and ready-made mixes. There follows a section of menus to make in 30 minutes.

I hope you will be able to make full use of all the time-saving ideas in this book. You will probably find that you can apply the short cuts to many recipes that you cook already. You can use this book to cook whole meals or just part of a meal. Remember though that new recipes, even the quickest, always take a little longer first time round.

STORE-CUPBOARD INGREDIENTS

CHECK LIST

*T*his is not meant to be a definitive list of ingredients to keep in stock, but it should help point you in the right direction. I have described how to cook, store and use some of them in the following section. Many of the items mentioned here can be kept for several months and, as they either cook quickly or need little preparation, they will help your 'Quick and Easy' repertoire. Another advantage of having a variety of ingredients available is that you can ring the changes easily to produce more interesting meals and liven-up leftovers when you're in a hurry. Basic standbys in the house save you having to make frequent shopping trips and a wide range of items on hand makes it easier to plan meals and cope with unexpected guests – but remember to restock as necessary.

Store cupboard
Grains: rice, buckwheat, bulgar wheat, millet
Flakes: porridge oats, crunchy granola cereal
Flour: wholemeal and cornmeal
Pasta: one or two varieties to serve with sauces
Pulses: lentils, split and whole, tinned varieties
Tofu: regular and silken
Nuts and seeds: two or three varieties (almonds, cashew, walnuts, peanuts, hazels), sesame and sunflower seeds
Peanut butter
Tahini
Dried fruit: mixed fruit salad, apricots, raisins
Oil: sunflower and olive
Vinegar: white wine
Concentrated apple juice
Tins of tomatoes and purée
Shoyu
Herbs, spices and seasonings – salt, pepper, garam masala, marjoram or oregano, paprika, turmeric and thyme are the most useful

Refrigerator
Eggs   Yoghurt
Hard cheese, cheddar type   Sour cream
Soft cheese, cottage, curd or ricotta   Margarine
Sugar-free jam   Fresh pasta

Freezer
Emergency vegetables: spinach, french beans, peas, sweetcorn
Ice cream and sorbet

Fresh products	Useful extras
Bread	Creamed coconut
Fruit	Fruit tinned in natural juice
Vegetables	Sugar-free relishes and chutneys

*H*ere is information on how to cook and store the quick-cooking whole-foods.

BUCKWHEAT

A small angular grain that is sold roasted or unroasted. You can tell the difference as the unroasted seeds are pale green and the roasted variety is a beige–brown colour.

To store: Buckwheat will keep at least a year if kept in a cool dry place.

To cook: Fry in a little oil, then add 2½ times the volume of boiling water, and simmer covered for 10–15 minutes. It is best left slightly undercooked and chewy.

Buckwheat can be cooked on its own or with onion, spices and other flavourings. Season at the end of cooking.

BULGAR WHEAT

A partially cooked cracked grain that, as the name implies, comes from wheat.

To store: Keep in a cool, dry place and use within six months.

To cook: Fry gently in a little oil, then pour over twice the volume of water and simmer for 8–10 minutes until just tender. To serve in salads, mix the grain with a little salt and soak in 2 or 2½ times the volume of boiling water, depending on how coarse it is, and leave for 15 minutes. Drain if necessary, then toss in a favourite vinaigrette.

MILLET

A golden-coloured, mild-flavoured grain.

To store: Millet will keep at least a year if kept in a cool, dry place.

To cook: Fry in a little oil, then add three times the volume of boiling water, and simmer covered for 20 minutes. Alternatively, pressure cook for 7 minutes.

Millet can be cooked on its own or with onion, spices and other flavourings. Season at the end of cooking.

RICE

Rice is available as long-grain and short-grain, and also as 'easy-cook', which has been par-boiled and so takes less time. Although you can use either white or brown rice in these recipes, I suggest you use brown – nutritionally it is far superior.

To store: Rice will keep for at least a year. Keep in a cool, dry place.

To cook: Bring twice the volume of water to the boil, add the rice, stir once or twice, then cover the pan and simmer. Short-grain rice takes 18–20 minutes; long-grain 20–25 minutes. At the end of this time, the water should be absorbed and the grain tender, though still chewy. Season at the end of cooking. Alternatively, rice can be cooked in a pressure cooker in 10 minutes.

To add more flavour, fry the rice in a little oil, with onion and spices if you wish, then pour on the correct amount of boiling water.

TOFU

Tofu, a product of the soya bean, is made from the curds of soya bean milk. When the whey is drained off, the curds can be pressed heavily to form regular tofu, a firm substance that can be easily cut into cubes. If gently pressed the end result is silken tofu which is easily mashed or puréed.

To store: While still in their packets, both regular and silken tofu have long shelf lives, but firm tofu should be stored in the refrigerator. Once the packets have been opened, keep any unused tofu in a bowl of fresh water in the refrigerator. It must be covered with water or a skin will develop. The water must be changed daily. It will keep like this for at least a week. If it has gone off, it will taste rather chalky. Tofu does not freeze satisfactorily.

To cook: Firm or regular tofu should be used for casseroles, stir-fries, marinades, kebabs and any other dish where it is important the pieces don't break apart. It is essential the tofu is either marinated for several hours to absorb flavour, or when saving time, fried with spices and other flavourings, or fried and then cooked in a tasty sauce.

Silken tofu is most suitable for dips, dressings and any dishes where a creamy texture is called for. It does not need to be cooked, but will only be successful when mixed with other well-flavoured ingredients as it has little taste of its own.

LENTILS

Sold as whole (brown and green) and split (red), lentils are the quickest cooking of the pulses. They do not need to be soaked.

To store: Keep in a cool, dry place and use within a year.

To cook: Pick them over for sticks and stones, then rinse well.

Cook red lentils in twice the volume of water if you need them to break down to a purée for bakes, burgers or pâtés. Use more water for soup. They will cook in 10–15 minutes.

Whole lentils need plenty of water. Cover them by at least 2 in. (5 cm.) and bring to the boil in a large pan. (A teaspoon of oil will help to prevent the water from boiling over.) Cover the pan and simmer for 30–40 minutes. If you are using a pressure cooker they should only need 10 minutes. Drain and use the cooking liquid as stock.

PULSES

These are a useful addition to any vegetarian diet. Pulses prepared from scratch need to be soaked for several hours: do large batches as, once cooked, pulses can be kept in the freezer for several months. However it is best to have some tinned pulses in your store cupboard for immediate use. Some of the most useful are red kidney beans, chick peas, haricot beans, black-eyed beans and cannellini beans. Most are readily available in supermarkets and health-food shops.

PASTA

Available now in many shapes, dried and fresh. Nutritionally, the best is wholemeal which makes a welcome change from bread or potatoes as a filler in a meal. It is very quick to prepare pasta as an accompaniment with most of the sauces mentioned in the chapter on One-pot Recipes.

To store: Fresh pasta must be kept in the refrigerator and used within 2–3 days. Dried pasta will keep 3 months in a cool dry place.

To cook: Whether fresh or dry, pasta needs plenty of water – at least 5 pints (3 litres) for 12 oz (350 g) pasta. Bring the water to the boil, then add salt and a little oil. Add the pasta and simmer until just soft but not soggy. Fresh pasta takes 4–5 minutes; dried pasta 8–12 minutes depending on the size. Drain well and serve immediately.

DRIED FRUIT

There are a large number of dried fruits available. They are extremely useful for creating quick puddings and for adding virtually instant flavour and colour to many savoury dishes. Have in stock a packet of mixed dried fruits or fruit 'salad', as these make excellent compotes which need virtually no preparation. Apricots and raisins, or sultanas, are probably the next most useful. Then for variety keep one or two of the following: dates, figs, peaches, Hunza apricots, large seeded raisins, or prunes.

To buy and store: Choose plump specimens and avoid those that have been coated with oil or have added sugar. Dried fruit will keep at least six months in an airtight container.

To cook: To reconstitute, plump up smaller fruits such as raisins in hot water (or fruit juice) for 5 minutes. For larger fruits, either stew whole for 30–40 minutes in a covered pan using plenty of liquid, or soak overnight. They can then be eaten as they are or cooked for a further 15–20 minutes. When cooking fruit to purée, cut it into small pieces as this will reduce the cooking time.

Dried fruit can also be reconstituted in the microwave: larger pieces of fruit need about 1 pint (600 ml) water or other liquid to 4 oz (125 g) fruit. Cook in a covered dish for 6–10 minutes. For best results leave to stand for 10–15 minutes for the flavours to develop.

EGGS AND DAIRY PRODUCTS

Dairy products and eggs are invaluable for creating quick meals. Eggs can be used to make omelettes and savoury custards, baked with vegetables, scrambled with peppers and tomatoes, hard-boiled and served sliced on top of rice or other grains, or served with salad.

Hard cheese can be quickly grated to make instantly appealing toppings and pizzas, stirred into sauces, mixed with cooked lentils for croquettes and loaves, or used for salad. Soft cheeses, such as cottage cheese, quark, cream cheese and ricotta, make smooth sauces, dips and dressings, quiche and pie fillings and, when sweetened, can be added to fresh or dried fruit or used as the base for many puddings.

Dairy products (yoghurt, crème fraîche, sour cream and cream) are useful for instant sauces and dips, toppings for puddings or the basis of a creamy dessert, dressing for salads, finishing off casseroles and soups.

To store: Hard cheese, cottage cheese and other soft cheese will often keep for 5–7 days or more, but check the details on the packet. Ricotta generally has a much shorter shelf life. Keep cheeses in the refrigerator, except when you are intending to provide a cheese board – then the cheese needs to be at room temperature.

Cream, yoghurt and sour cream can also be kept several days. If you only shop once a week, use the dairy produce early on.

Keep eggs in a cool place such as the refrigerator, and these will also last several days.

VEGETABLES

Most vegetables are certainly quick to cook and they add colour and texture to many dishes. As they are not very sustaining in themselves, an obvious exception being the potato, they do need to be served with other ingredients such as grains, beans or pasta to make a proper meal. The main drawback with vegetables is that they do not keep long, so it is not always possible to have a great variety on hand unless you spend more time shopping. Here are a few notes about buying and storing vegetables – but do note that the longer you keep them, the more vitamins you lose.

Buying and storing: When buying vegetables, try to shop for them in small quantities so you can get fresh supplies. This may mean that you will have to make more shopping trips, however, so if you can't spare the time, do make sure that you buy better quality products as they will deteriorate less quickly. With root vegetables and vegetable fruits such as courgettes, look for firm specimens. Peppers and aubergines should have glossy skins. Don't buy green vegetables or brassicas that are slightly yellow in colour or have wilted leaves. Once home, remove any polythene wrappings and store them in a cool, dry place or in the refrigerator to keep them fresh. (Better still, avoid buying products wrapped in polythene.)

Most salad ingredients, especially lettuce and watercress, wilt quickly. Other items, such as Chinese leaves, Iceberg lettuce, spring onions and radish, will keep for 2–3 days in the refrigerator.

Green vegetables and vegetable fruits – particularly peppers, courgettes and aubergines – will keep longer, but do store them in the refrigerator and try to use them within a week. Cauliflower, cabbage and celery keep well too, but broccoli soon loses its colour. Mushrooms should be kept dry and stored in a cool place. Tomatoes and avocados, if bought slightly under-ripe, can be left at room temperature to ripen.

Root vegetables – carrots, turnips and the like, and onions – will keep in a dark, cool and well-ventilated place for up to 2 weeks and potatoes longer still.

To cook: Nutritionally it is best to steam, stir-fry or microwave, but whichever method you choose you should always try to cut the pieces the same size so that they cook evenly.

When steaming, remember that the water underneath should be boiling fiercely. Use plenty of water so the pan doesn't boil dry and you don't need to keep checking on it.

Some notes on stir-frying are on page 58.

If you are using a microwave, you should err on the side of under-cooking as the vegetables will continue cooking once removed from the microwave. The exact timing will vary depending on what you cook and how much. As a general guideline, you should add 2–3 tablespoons water to the vegetables and cover the dish. 1 lb (450 g) may take somewhere between 6–12 minutes. You should also allow a little standing time once the vegetables are removed from the microwave.

When using vegetables, contrast colour or texture wherever possible: in this way even a simple mixture can make a good, attractive dish. You don't need a huge variety in every meal. If you have used a number of vegetables in a main course, pulses make a good side dish. Use a tinned variety and pep them up with some fresh herbs, garlic or lemon juice.

QUICK STARTERS

*W*hy bother with starters when you are trying to save time, you might ask. Contrary to what you might expect, starters needn't always mean extra work. They can often replace the need for a side dish, as a separate course makes the meal seem more extensive. This gives you, the cook, time to relax if you've rushed round making a last-minute meal, and it also gives the main course more time to cook.

Starters often consist of easy ideas that can be augmented to make full meals – ideal for mid-week suppers when time is scarce – and in this chapter I've included a short range of recipes that you can use in this way.

There are three soups as these not only make a welcome start to any meal, but when served with a good hunk of bread, some cheese and a little salad can make an easy and nutritious meal in themselves. For speed, these can all be cooked in a pressure cooker. (If you are new to this gadget, do read the notes given on page 65.) One of the soups is based on a root vegetable purée which is a trouble-free way of making a creamy soup; another is enriched with seeds, a good device to add flavour; and finally I've used split peas as they are amongst the quickest to cook in the pulse family. (A substantial ingredient such as this makes more of a meal in a bowl.) If you are cooking soups in a hurry, I suggest that, in addition to using the pressure cooker, you also purée them either fully or partially, as this blends the flavours. Soups freeze well, so try and make extra quantities when you have time. If you are able to prepare them in advance, they will benefit from reheating. I like to make a soup at the beginning of the day, and leave it as the basis for a meal that evening.

I've also included a recipe for a simple vegetable starter, Lemon and Coriander Courgettes. This is quick to prepare, and can be served hot or cold. The same idea can be used with a great variety of vegetables, and you can alter the flavours in the dressing. This type of delicately flavoured starter is useful to begin a robust meal.

Dips and pâtés make simple and popular starters, or fill out a buffet or salad meal. The two ideas given here can literally be made in minutes. For speed serve them with bread or crackers. If you have more time prepare a selection of colourful raw vegetables. When served like this, they can take quite a time to eat – useful if you find you need extra minutes for the main course to cook!

Fresh fruit is a light way to begin a meal and suits nearly every occasion. Below are some quick tips where I've suggested a couple of combinations; the recipe section also includes a delicious cream and walnut dressing to serve with pears – simple to assemble and a refreshing start (or finish) to any meal.

QUICK TIPS

* Try different simple combinations of fruit: melon and raspberries, or pawpaw sprinkled with lime juice, or grapefruit mixed with slices of stem ginger.
* Savoury snacks, such as Japanese crackers or curried chick peas, make good pre-prandial nibbles.
* Pineapple, fresh or in its own juices, is delicious with a spoonful of cottage cheese sprinkled with paprika.
* Avocado served with either raspberry vinegar or shoyu and black pepper is unusual but interesting.
* A plain steamed vegetable can be turned into a quick appetiser tossed in garlic with a little butter or French dressing.
* Serve freshly cooked pasta, tossed in a little cream, as a starter.
* Good quality ranges of bottled fruit and vegetable cocktails are now readily available and useful to keep in stock.
* Serve a side salad as a starter instead of with the main course.
* Shop-bought pâtés (olive is a particularly good variety and keeps well) can be served with crackers.
* Good-quality mayonnaise can be used as a dip with raw vegetables.

MELLOW PARSNIP SOUP

*R*oot vegetables, such as parsnips, carrots and swede, purée well to make colourful creamy soups. These are cheap and quick to make. Spices add a good flavour that will invariably improve if the soup is made in advance and reheated.

MAKES 1¾ pints (1 litre)

1 tablespoon sunflower oil
1 onion, peeled and finely chopped
1 clove garlic, crushed
½ teaspoon ground cinnamon
½ teaspoon ground ginger
½ teaspoon turmeric
1 lb (450 g) parsnips, peeled and diced
1 pint (600 ml) vegetable stock
Juice of ½ lemon
Salt and black pepper

Gently heat the oil and cook the onion for 2–3 minutes, then add the garlic and spices and cook for 2 minutes. Add the diced parsnips and cook over a low heat for 10 minutes. Add the stock and simmer for 45 minutes or pressure cook for 15 minutes. Leave to cool, then purée adding the lemon juice and a little more stock if necessary. Season to taste, and reheat before serving.

CELERY AND SUNFLOWER SOUP

*A*dding nuts or seeds to a soup increases the protein content as well as enriching the mixture and giving it a creamy texture when blended. Celery and sunflower seeds both have quite strong flavours and complement each other well in this soup.

MAKES 2 pints (1.2 litres)

1 tablespoon sunflower oil
1 onion, peeled and finely
   chopped
8 oz (225 g) celery, diced
4 oz (125 g) sunflower seeds

1¼ pints (750 ml) vegetable
   stock or water
1 teaspoon dill weed
1 bay leaf
Salt and black pepper
5 fl oz (150 ml) natural yoghurt

Heat the oil and gently fry the onion for 3 minutes. Add the celery and sunflower seeds and cook for 2 minutes, stirring well so the seeds toast slightly. Pour over the boiling vegetable stock or water and add the herbs. Bring the soup to the boil, then simmer gently for 30 minutes or pressure cook for 10 minutes.

Leave the soup to cool slightly, then blend until quite smooth. Season to taste. Add the yoghurt, then reheat gently before serving.

This soup is also delicious served chilled.

GREEN SPLIT PEA AND ONION SOUP

*P*ulses – that is beans, peas and lentils – all make good soups as their floury nature acts as a natural thickening agent. Split peas are quick-cooking and do not need to be soaked in advance – although if you have time, it will help them to soften if you soak them for an hour or so in hot water. You can then cut down on the cooking time by 15 minutes, or by 5 minutes if you are using a pressure cooker.

MAKES 2 pints (1.2 litres)

1 tablespoon sunflower oil
1 onion, peeled and finely chopped
8 oz (225 g) swede, grated
4 sticks celery, chopped
6 oz (175 g) green split peas
1½ pints (900 ml) onion stock made with a stock cube
1 teaspoon mustard powder
Salt and black pepper

Heat the oil and gently fry the onion for 3 minutes. Add the swede, celery and green split peas, stir well and cook for 5 minutes. Pour over the stock and add the mustard powder. Bring the liquid to the boil, then cover the pan and simmer for 1 hour, or pressure cook for 20 minutes.

Leave to cool slightly, then blend until smooth. Season to taste. Re-heat and serve with granary or rye bread.

AVOCADO DIP

*T*he rich buttery quality of an avocado blends well with the sharp flavour of crème fraîche or soured cream, and it's easy to make with a blender or food processor. As avocado flesh discolours rapidly, you need to make this dip shortly before serving – although the fruit can be bought several days in advance and left to ripen in the warmth of the kitchen if necessary.

SERVES 4

1 ripe avocado
2 tablespoons crème fraîche or
  sour cream

1 clove garlic, crushed
Juice of ½ lemon
A few drops of tabasco
Salt and black pepper

Blend all the ingredients together until quite smooth. Season to taste.

Serve as a dip with peppers, baby sweetcorn, and corn chips within 30 minutes of making.

LEMON AND CORIANDER COURGETTES

*T*his simple vegetable dish can be presented in a number of different ways, either hot or cold as a starter, or as a side vegetable with a main course such as Nice Spice Rice (page 28) or Peppers stuffed with Mushrooms and Nuts (page 46). The recipe also works well with fresh broad beans or runner beans.

SERVES 4

1 lb (450 g) courgettes, trimmed
  and roughly chopped
Juice of ½ lemon

1 tablespoon olive oil
1–2 tablespoons coriander
  leaves, chopped
1 clove garlic, crushed
Salt and black pepper

Prepare the courgettes and either steam them until just soft (about 6 minutes) or microwave them for 6–7 minutes. Do err on the side of under-cooking as they will then retain a slightly crunchy texture.

Mix together the remaining ingredients and toss into the hot courgettes. Season to taste. Serve with bread and butter.

PEARS WITH CREAM AND WALNUT DRESSING

*T*he dressing and walnut coating for this delicious starter can be prepared several hours in advance, leaving you a short last-minute job of assembly. Alternatively, prepare and coat the pears but don't slice them until just before serving. With this method, you can leave them prepared for an hour in the refrigerator. The success of the recipe depends on the quality of the fruit used. Choose Williams pears, but avoid over-ripe ones that may be brown in the centre.

SERVES 4

½ oz (10 g) walnuts, chopped
1 tablespoon wheatgerm

2 large pears
Cress or watercress for garnish

For the dressing:
2 tablespoons thick double cream
Juice of ½ lemon
2 oz (50 g) cream cheese
2 teaspoons concentrated apple juice or honey

Mix the walnuts and wheatgerm together and toast in the microwave for 1 minute. Alternatively, place under the grill and toast for 2–3 minutes, shaking frequently. Grind the mixture until the nuts are the consistency of breadcrumbs.

In a separate bowl, mix together the remaining ingredients for the dressing and beat until smooth.

Peel the pears, halve and core. Place cut side down on small plates and coat with the dressing. Sprinkle liberally with the toasted walnut mixture. Just before serving, cut into slices and allow the slices to fall sideways and fan out slightly. Garnish with cress or watercress and serve immediately.

PEANUT AND CUMIN PÂTÉ

*N*uts have a high fat content, which means they make a good basis for a pâté or spread. Their flavour is improved if you roast them first and this is an extremely quick process in a microwave. If you use a conventional oven or grill instead, do keep checking on the nuts so they brown evenly. The cumin used in this recipe adds a slightly aromatic flavour which complements the nuts. This pâté will keep for 3–4 days in the fridge, but should be covered as it tends to dry out.

SERVES 4

4 oz (125 g) peanuts
1 teaspoon cumin seeds
1 tablespoon peanut butter

1 medium dessert apple
1–2 teaspoons concentrated apple juice
Salt and black pepper

Roast the peanuts in the microwave for 4–5 minutes, shaking the dish occasionally. Add the cumin seeds and roast for a further minute. Alternatively put the nuts in the oven to roast. Set the oven at gas 5, 375°F (190°C) and put the peanuts in for 10 minutes, then add the cumin seeds and roast for 2 minutes.

Leave to cool slightly, then using a liquidiser or the steel blade of a food processor, blend with the remaining ingredients until fairly smooth. Season to taste. Serve with bread, toast or biscuits. Alternatively, use as a stuffing for dates or celery sticks.

HEALTHY WHOLEFOODS

*A*s you'll have seen from the suggested list for your store cupboard, you should keep a range of quick-cooking grains, pulses, nuts and seeds to complement vegetable and dairy ingredients and be a quick means of providing the substance of a meal. Some of these foods, such as bulgar wheat or tofu, may be unfamiliar, but they are worth getting to know as they will enable you to make wholesome food quickly. There are explanatory notes about these and other ingredients in chapter one.

In this recipe section, I've devised a number of dishes for easy-to-make main courses using these staple foods mixed with a number of different ingredients. I've started the chapter with a colourful rice dish which can be served on its own or as part of a more elaborate meal.

Another group of staple ingredients that act as fast foods are lentils, either whole or split, and the hot-pot in this chapter is a versatile warming meal. (There are more lentil recipes in the chapter on sauces.)

This chapter also contains two recipes for bulgar wheat. The first is an extremely simple pilaff cooked with nuts and dried fruit. The second idea uses a bulgar and vegetable filling as a bake with a topping of yoghurt – an idea you could certainly use on other grain or vegetable bakes.

Two more unusual grains that are very quick-cooking are millet and buckwheat. The former is very popular with children, as it has a mild flavour and creamy texture; the latter has a stronger flavour, so it works well when cooked with other well-flavoured ingredients. It has an excellent light texture for a bake or savoury slice.

Tofu is becoming increasingly available, but it is still a mystery to many people. It must be one of the most convenient wholesome ingredients. As you'll find from trying out the two recipes in this chapter, the secret lies in giving it a chance to absorb flavours.

QUICK TIPS

* Cook grains in stock to add flavour.
* Purée some onion with spices and fry this with a grain to add extra flavour before cooking.
* Once cooked, add a vinaigrette, plain lemon juice, or yoghurt to grains, pasta, or lentils to change their flavour and appearance.
* Left-over grains and pasta keep well, will freeze, reheat easily in the microwave.
* Left-over grain and lentil dishes make a good basis for burgers and vegetable stuffings.
* A few tablespoons of bulgar wheat can be added to a casserole 10 minutes before the end of cooking to add texture and substance.
* Steep lentils and split peas in boiling water while you are assembling other ingredients to cut down the cooking time still further.
* Use saffron or a little turmeric to liven up a plain grain dish.
* Have tins of beans and lentils in stock. Look out for packets of grain mixtures.
* Tofu does not keep for long, so if you have any pieces left over it is best to purée them into a soup or mash them into a casserole.

NICE SPICE RICE

*T*his rice dish can be served as a simple main course with an extra vegetable such as steamed broccoli, buttered carrots, or Lemon and Coriander Courgettes (page 22). The mixture of grain, seeds and peas is nutritionally very good as these ingredients make a meal full of protein.

For a more elaborate meal, serve with Creamed Red Lentil and Coconut Sauce (page 75) or Simple Vegetable Sauce (page 73), or a vegetable dish such as Spinach, Pine Kernel and Sultana Stir-fry (page 61).

You could make this recipe with barley, wheat or buckwheat instead of rice, but you would need to adjust the cooking time and liquid content according to what you choose (see page 11).

SERVES 4

1 tablespoon olive oil
1 onion, peeled and finely
    chopped
1 clove garlic, crushed
8 oz (225 g) long-grain brown
    rice or mixed grains
1 teaspoon turmeric

½ teaspoon chilli powder
1 pint (600 ml) boiling water
8 oz (225 g) fresh or frozen
    peas
2 oz (50 g) mixed seeds
    (sesame, sunflower, and
    pumpkin)
2 teaspoons shoyu
Salt and black pepper

Heat the oil and gently fry the onion for 3 minutes. Add the garlic, rice or grains and spices and fry for a further 3 minutes, stirring occasionally so that the grains do not stick. Pour over the boiling water and stir once, then add the peas. Bring back to the boil, cover the pan and simmer for 25–30 minutes or until the grains are well cooked.

While the grains are cooking, lightly toast the seeds in a frying pan for a few minutes or in the microwave for 2 minutes. Coat in shoyu and then cook for a further minute. Add these flavoured seeds to the rice about 5 minutes before the end of the cooking time.

Season to taste, and serve hot.

MIXED LENTIL HOT-POT

*L*entils are an invaluable ingredient for casseroles. They provide substance and protein, have a good earthy flavour and are one of the few members of the pulse family that don't need to be soaked before being cooked. I like to use a mixture of lentils as I find the whole ones (green and brown) add texture, whilst the split red variety cook down to a purée and help thicken the stew. The time given is the minimum for cooking this dish; I would advise you to cook it for longer if possible as the flavour and texture go on improving. If you substitute other vegetables for the peppers, add a teaspoon of paprika as its sweetness lifts the floury quality of the pulses. This dish will keep 3–4 days in the refrigerator, and can be frozen for several months. Serve with a baked potato or pasta or, for a lighter meal, a green vegetable. Leftovers make good pasty fillings.

SERVES 4

1 tablespoon sunflower oil
1 onion, peeled and finely
  chopped
1 clove garlic, crushed
2 large peppers, red or green,
  de-seeded and chopped
8 oz (225 g) mangetout, roughly
  chopped
8 oz (225 g) mixed lentils (red,
  green and brown), washed
2 pints (1.2 litres) onion stock
2 tablespoons tomato purée
2 tablespoons shoyu
Salt and black pepper

Heat the oil and gently fry the onion for 3 minutes, then add the garlic and cook for 2 minutes. Add the vegetables and lentils to the pan and stir well. Cook for 3 minutes. Pour over the boiling stock and stir in the tomato purée and shoyu. Bring the mixture to pressure, then simmer for 15–20 minutes. Leave to cool, then season to taste. Reheat if necessary before serving.

Note: This recipe can also be cooked in a conventional saucepan, but it does take quite a lot longer – the hot-pot needs to be simmered for 1–1½ hours. However the actual preparation time is relatively quick and the pot can be left bubbling away while you get on with something else.

PERSIAN PILAFF

*B*ulgar wheat is a very versatile grain, equally good hot or cold. It can be combined with a variety of ingredients: vegetables such as peppers, mushrooms, carrots and courgettes; dried fruits such as raisins or currants, and most nuts and seeds. Here I have cooked it with cashews and apricots and the aromatic spice mixture garam masala. As with most of these all-in-one grain dishes, it can be eaten by itself for a basic supper, or served with extra vegetables and salad, or accompany a casserole.

SERVES 4

1 tablespoon olive oil
3 spring onions, chopped
1 clove garlic, crushed
1 teaspoon garam masala

2 oz (50 g) cashew pieces
2 oz (50 g) dried apricots, cut in slivers
8 oz (225 g) bulgar wheat
1 pint (600 ml) vegetable stock
Salt and black pepper

Heat the oil and gently fry the spring onions for 3 minutes, then add the garlic and cook for another minute. Stir in the garam masala and cashew nuts and fry these for 2 minutes so that the cashews brown slightly. Then add the apricots and bulgar wheat, cook for 1 minute and pour over the boiling stock. Cover the pan and cook the mixture over a low heat for 10 minutes. By this time all the water should be absorbed and the bulgar wheat tender. If not, add a little more water and cook for a couple more minutes. Season well and serve hot or cold.

BULGAR WHEAT BAKE

*T*his recipe is a more elaborate version of a pilaff as the mixture is finished off by being covered with a tangy lemon and yoghurt topping which sets as it bakes. It turns this recipe into a most presentable supper or lunch dish which could be accompanied by a simple salad and some extra yoghurt or Tzatziki (page 125). The yoghurt topping is not suitable for freezing, but you could freeze the filling and add the topping at a later stage.

SERVES 4

1 tablespoon olive oil
1 onion, peeled and finely chopped
1 clove garlic, crushed
1 large red or green pepper, de-seeded and diced
4 oz (100 g) bulgar wheat
½ teaspoon ground cinnamon

1 × 14 oz (400g) tin of tomatoes, puréed
1 tablespoon shoyu
5 fl oz (150 ml) vegetable stock
Salt and black pepper
1 × 7 oz (200 g) carton Greek yoghurt
1 egg
Juice of ½ lemon

Pre-heat the oven to gas mark 5, 375°F (190°C).

Heat the oil and gently fry the onion for 3 minutes, then add the garlic and pepper and cook for 5 minutes. Add the bulgar wheat and cinnamon, stir in well, then pour over the puréed tomatoes. Add the shoyu, then bring the mixture to the boil. Cover the pan and simmer for 10 minutes, adding the vegetable stock if necessary as the bulgar wheat will absorb a large amount of liquid. Season to taste. Spoon the mixture into an oiled ovenproof dish.

In a separate bowl, mix together the yoghurt, egg and lemon juice. Pour this over the top of the bulgar wheat. Bake for 20–25 minutes or until the topping has set. Serve hot.

MILLET AND TOMATO GRATIN

*M*illet is somewhat different to the other grains in that it tends to cook to a much softer consistency, so the end result is more pudding-like in texture. It is, nonetheless, delicious and popular with children who like the mild flavour. Any gratin that is left over is excellent shaped into small burgers and shallow-fried: serve these with some freshly made tomato sauce and you have an extra meal with very little trouble. You can also make this dish without cheese by substituting chopped nuts or seeds and then grilling them on top until they are lightly toasted.

SERVES 4

1 tablespoon sunflower oil
1 onion, finely chopped
8 oz (225 g) carrots, diced
6 oz (175 g) millet
1 teaspoon dried thyme

1 × 14 oz (400 g) tin of
    tomatoes, puréed
Water or vegetable stock
1 teaspoon miso
Salt and black pepper
6 oz (175 g) Cheddar cheese,
    grated

Heat the oil and gently fry the onion for 2–3 minutes. Add the carrots and sweat over a low heat for 5 minutes, then stir in the millet and thyme. Cook for 2 minutes so that the grains toast slightly.

Prepare the tomatoes and make the liquid up to 1 pint (600 ml) using either water or vegetable stock. Dissolve the miso in 2 tablespoons water and mix into the tomato liquid. Pour this over the millet mixture. Bring the liquid to the boil, then cover the pan and simmer for 30–35 minutes or until the millet is cooked. Check on the water content towards the end of the cooking time and add a little more if necessary. Do not stir too often or the millet will become very sticky. Season to taste.

Spoon the mixture into a lightly oiled 7-inch (18-cm) tin and level out. Then cover with grated cheese and grill for 3 minutes or until the cheese has just melted and browned slightly. Serve hot.

Opposite: Nice Spice Rice (page 28) and Lemon and Coriander Courgettes (page 22)
Overleaf: Mellow Parsnip Soup (page 19) and Pears with Cream and Walnut Dressing (page 23)

BUCKWHEAT AND RED LENTIL BAKE

*B*uckwheat and red lentils can be cooked together in the same pan as they are ready in roughly the same time. This saves effort and washing up! The two ingredients combine well as buckwheat has a strong flavour which is diluted by the lentils, yet its springy texture is not lost. This roast is mixed with mushrooms and pepper but carrots, parsnips and shredded cabbage would work equally well. The bake will firm up in texture as it stands and, although designed to be eaten hot, is good cold. It can be frozen and reheats well, especially in the microwave. Serve it with Pine Kernel and Tomato Sauce (page 72) or Peanut and Sesame Sauce (page 76).

SERVES 4

4 oz (125 g) buckwheat
3 oz (75 g) red lentils
1 pint (600 ml) boiling water
1 tablespoon olive oil
1 onion, peeled and finely chopped
1 teaspoon dried thyme
1 teaspoon paprika
¹/₄ teaspoon chilli powder
8 oz (225 g) mushrooms, wiped and sliced
1 green pepper, de-seeded and diced
1 × 7 oz (200 g) tin of tomatoes, puréed
1 tablespoon tomato purée
1 tablespoon shoyu
Salt and black pepper

Pre-heat the oven to gas mark 5, 375°F (190°C).

Put the buckwheat and lentils into a saucepan, pour over the boiling water, bring to the boil and cover. Simmer for 8–10 minutes or until the liquid is absorbed and the buckwheat and lentils just cooked.

In a separate pan, heat the oil and gently fry the onion for 2 minutes, then add the herbs and spices and cook for 1 minute. Add the mushrooms and green pepper to the pan. Cook for 5 minutes.

In a large bowl, mix together the cooked buckwheat, lentils, vegetables, and stir in the tomatoes, tomato purée and shoyu. Season to taste.

Spoon the mixture into a lightly greased ovenproof dish and bake in the oven for 30 minutes. Alternatively, microwave on full power for 8–10 minutes. Serve hot.

TOFU IN A BARBECUE SAUCE

*T*ofu needs to be marinated, or cooked in a tasty sauce, to give it a chance to absorb flavours. This recipe should be made using firm or regular tofu, and if you wish could be made in the microwave. If you make it in advance, it reheats well and the flavours will become stronger.

Serve with a plain grain accompaniment and a simple steamed vegetable or a stir-fry vegetable mixture.

SERVES 4

1 tablespoon olive oil
1 onion, peeled and finely chopped
1 clove garlic, crushed
12 oz (350 g) firm tofu, cubed
1 tablespoon shoyu
1 teaspoon tabasco

1 × 14 oz (400 g) tin of tomatoes, puréed
1 tablespoon tomato purée
2 tablespoons concentrated apple juice
2 slices of lemon
1 bay leaf
½ teaspoon celery seed
Salt and black pepper

Heat the oil and gently fry the onion for 3 minutes, then add the garlic, tofu, shoyu and tabasco. Fry these ingredients for several minutes so that the tofu becomes fairly crisp. Turn the cubes over carefully so they do not break apart.

Add the remaining ingredients, cover the pan and simmer gently for 15–20 minutes. Season to taste. Serve hot.

MARINATED TOFU

*T*his recipe works on the same principle as the previous one where the tofu is mixed with strong flavours to give it some taste. Here the flavours are Oriental with the combination of ginger, shoyu and aniseed. To save time the tofu is cooked in the marinade but then fried briefly to give the pieces a crisp texture. This dish needs to be served with a grain such as rice, or noodles to make a meal. It is also excellent with stir-fry vegetables. If you prefer, the tofu can be left for several hours in the marinade and then drained and fried with the marinade heated separately.

SERVES 4

12 oz–1 lb (350–450 g) tofu

For the marinade:
4 tablespoons lemon juice
6 tablespoons water

4 tablespoons shoyu
2 tablespoons tomato purée
1 × 14 oz (400 g) tin of
   tomatoes, puréed
2 tablespoons honey
2 teaspoons root ginger, grated
2 cloves garlic, crushed
2 teaspoons aniseed

Mix all the ingredients for the marinade together. Cut the tofu into small pieces and put in a small pan. Pour over the marinade. Heat the mixture gently, turning the pieces of tofu over carefully so they do not break apart, and cook the sauce for 10 minutes. Drain the pieces carefully and continue cooking the sauce on a low heat.

In a separate pan, heat a little oil and fry the tofu for 3–4 minutes so the pieces crisp up slightly.

Serve the tofu hot, with the marinade poured over the top.

MAINLY VEGETABLES

*T*his chapter concentrates on main courses in which vegetables are the most important ingredient. You'll also find notes in the introductory section of the book about buying and storing vegetables, as well as some tips about vegetable cookery generally.

Vegetables can be presented in many different ways. I've started the section with a simple mixture of softened vegetables covered with melted cheese which is both easy and colourful and can be made with more or less anything you have on hand. There are two simple stews – the Spanish-style Cacerolita and an easy Red Cabbage Casserole – plus a couple of ideas for baking vegetables in the oven. Presentation is always important in cookery, and serving vegetables whole with a tasty stuffing is an easy way of making an attractive dish. I've included here a quick recipe for Peppers stuffed with Mushrooms and Nuts. The chapter finishes with some stir-fries – here you really can save time with the cooking and even the preparation needn't be lengthy. There is some information about stir-frying in general just before this section.

QUICK TIPS

* Dress plain vegetables with a quick sauce for the basis of a simple meal.
* Remember the most successful combinations of vegetables will have some contrast of colour, texture and flavour.
* Simple, but unusual, mixtures make good meals served with grains or pasta. Try curried carrots with oranges and raisins.
* Make a purée of one vegetable to serve with another: broccoli purée is good with cauliflower, carrot purée with green beans.
* Use left-over vegetable mixtures to fill pancakes, as pie fillings or as stuffings for vegetables such as peppers.
* Use chopped nuts and seeds as quick toppings to add texture.
* Blend a cold cooked vegetable into mayonnaise or yoghurt for unusual and more substantial salad dressings.
* Chop vegetables in different ways to add variety.
* Have on hand some frozen vegetables for emergencies. Peas, beans and spinach are most useful.
* Add a tin of beans to a vegetable stew for protein and substance.

LAYERED CHEESY VEGETABLES

*L*ightly cooked mixtures of vegetables can be turned into a quick meal if layered with cheese and grilled. Serve with a good wholemeal bread and you have an excellent supper. This recipe is also an interesting way of serving vegetables as a side dish.

SERVES 4

1 tablespoon sunflower oil
1 onion, peeled and finely chopped
4 sticks celery, washed and diced
1 lb (450 g) courgettes, trimmed and chopped
2 red peppers, de-seeded and chopped
1 teaspoon mixed herbs
2–3 drops tabasco
Salt and black pepper
6 oz (175 g) vegetarian Edam cheese, grated

Heat the oil and gently fry the onion for 3 minutes. Add the vegetables and stir in well. Cover the pan and cook the mixture over a gentle heat for 10 minutes or until the vegetables are just soft.

Remove the pan from the heat and sprinkle over the herbs and tabasco. Season to taste.

Put half the vegetables in a shallow ovenproof dish, cover with half the grated cheese, then add the remaining vegetables and sprinkle on the rest of the cheese. Put under the grill and cook for 3–4 minutes or until the cheese melts and browns. Serve hot.

CACEROLITA

*T*his is an easily made tasty vegetable ragoût with the familiar red and green look of many Spanish-style dishes. Extra flavour is added with toasted almonds, sun-dried tomatoes and a little chilli. You can of course use a range of other vegetables in season, or frozen sweetcorn or green beans.

SERVES 4

2 oz (50 g) almonds
1 tablespoon olive oil
1 onion, finely chopped
1 clove garlic, crushed
1 teaspoon cumin seeds
1 large red pepper, de-seeded
  and sliced
1 large green pepper, de-seeded
  and sliced

12 oz (350 g) button
  mushrooms, sliced
¼ teaspoon chilli powder
2 teaspoons fresh oregano,
  chopped
2 tablespoons sun-dried tomato
  paste
1 tablespoon tomato purée
¼ pint (150 ml) vegetable stock
8 oz (225 g) peas
Salt and pepper

Roast the almonds in the oven at gas mark 6, 400°F (200°C) for 7 minutes or in the microwave for 2–3 minutes. Then chop roughly.

Heat the olive oil and gently fry the onion for 3 minutes until just softening. Add the garlic and cumin seeds and fry for 3 minutes or until the cumin is well roasted. Then add the prepared vegetables and chilli powder and mix in well. Next stir in the chopped almonds, oregano, sun-dried tomatoes, tomato purée and stock. Bring to the boil and simmer covered for 30 minutes. Then add the peas and cook for another 5 minutes until they are tender. Season to taste and serve with rice, chunks of bread, or jacket potatoes.

RED CABBAGE CASSEROLE

*R*ed cabbage is one of the few vegetables that I really enjoy over-cooked! It keeps its colour and a good texture and I like to serve it with jacket potatoes and soured cream. If you want a more elaborate meal, make the Creamed Potato Savoury (page 93) as an accompaniment. A variety of vegetables can be cooked with red cabbage – the peppery flavour of turnip works particularly well. A few sunflower seeds add an interesting touch. This dish can be frozen, and will also keep well in the refrigerator for 3–4 days.

SERVES 4

1 tablespoon sunflower oil
1 lb (450 g) leeks, finely
  shredded
1½ lb (750 g) red cabbage,
  finely shredded
1 lb (450 g) turnips, finely
  shredded

2 oz (50 g) sunflower seeds
2 tablespoons concentrated
  apple juice
2 tablespoons red wine vinegar
1 teaspoon mustard grains
Salt and black pepper

Heat the oil and stir-fry the vegetables for 5 minutes with the sunflower seeds. Then add the concentrated apple juice, wine vinegar, mustard and 2 tablespoons water. Simmer for 45–50 minutes (or pressure cook for 10 minutes), leave to cool, then season well.

Serve either hot or cold.

CAULIFLOWER AND RICOTTA CHEESE PIE

*C*auliflower can be cooked extremely quickly if it is prepared in a food processor. It is a useful vegetable as its strong flavour complements egg and cheese mixtures which would otherwise be bland. This pie is made with cooked cauliflower baked with ricotta cheese and beaten egg. This dish could be served with green vegetables and new potatoes for a light easy meal.

SERVES 4

1 medium cauliflower, cut into thin slices
1 oz (25 g) butter
1 onion, peeled and finely chopped
1 tablespoon flour

1 teaspoon dried thyme
8 oz (225 g) ricotta cheese
4 eggs
2 oz (50 g) Parmesan cheese, grated
Salt and black pepper
Poppy seeds for garnish

Preheat the oven to gas mark 6, 400°F (200°C).

Steam the cauliflower for 6–7 minutes or microwave for 4–5 minutes until just tender. Set aside.

In a separate pan, gently melt the butter, then fry the onion for 3 minutes. Add the cooked cauliflower and stir in well. Sprinkle over the flour and thyme and cook for 1 minute.

Blend the ricotta with the eggs and Parmesan and season well, then mix in the cooked onion and cauliflower.

Spoon the mixture into a lightly greased ovenproof dish and garnish with a sprinkling of poppy seeds. Bake for 20 minutes. Serve hot.

RUSSIAN POTATO CASSEROLE WITH CARAWAY

*T*his is a light cheesy bake made with layers of raw vegetables covered with sauce. Obviously the vegetables can vary according to what is in season. You can save time with this recipe by making the sauce with the all-in-one method as described on page 108.

Serve this with a green vegetable or salad, or for something more substantial, some pulses such as red kidney beans in a sauce.

SERVES 4

1 oz (25 g) margarine or butter
1 oz (25 g) wholemeal flour
1 pint (600 ml) milk
1 lb (450 g) leeks, thinly sliced

4 medium potatoes, thinly sliced
12 oz (350 g) cottage cheese
1–2 teaspoons caraway seeds
Salt and black pepper

Pre-heat the oven to gas mark 5, 375°F (190°C).

Melt the margarine over a gentle heat, then stir in the flour to make a roux. Cook this for 2 minutes. Gradually add the milk, stirring all the time so the liquid blends in well and does not go lumpy. Bring the sauce to the boil and simmer gently for 3 minutes so that it thickens and the flour is properly cooked.

Lightly oil a large ovenproof dish. Layer the vegetables with the cottage cheese and sprinkle with caraway seeds. Season each layer and begin and end with potatoes.

Pour over the sauce, then bake for 50–55 minutes or until the potato is tender. Alternatively, microwave the bake on full power for 10–12 minutes and then brown under a conventional grill. Serve hot.

PEPPERS STUFFED WITH MUSHROOMS AND NUTS

Stuffed peppers always make a good colourful centrepiece for a meal. Preparing the peppers is not time-consuming, but they should be blanched as this helps them soften when they are baked. The stuffing I have chosen is quick but tasty and could easily be prepared in advance. Serve these with Broccoli and Blue Cheese Sauce (page 74) or Pine Kernel and Tomato Sauce (page 72) and rice for a tasty supper.

SERVES 4

4 medium-sized green peppers
1 tablespoon sunflower oil
1 onion, peeled and finely
  chopped
1 clove garlic, crushed

8 oz (225 g) mushrooms, wiped
  and diced
8 oz (225 g) mixed nuts,
  coarsely milled
2 tablespoons tomato purée
2 teaspoons dried marjoram
Salt and black pepper

Pre-heat the oven to gas mark 5, 375°F (190°C).

Wash the peppers and cut a lid from the top of each. Scoop out the seeds and any white membranes.

Bring a large pan of water to the boil and simmer the peppers for 3 minutes to soften them slightly.

Heat the oil and gently fry the onion for 3 minutes, then add the garlic and mushrooms and cook for a further 3 minutes. Stir in the nuts and cook for 1 minute. Remove the pan from the heat and mix in the remaining ingredients. Season to taste. Divide the mixture in four and fill each pepper. Place the stuffed peppers in an ovenproof dish and add 2–3 tablespoons stock or water. Bake for 20–25 minutes, then serve hot.

SIMPLE SALADS

*I*t is important to have some salads, or raw vegetables in your diet. They are an excellent source of vitamins and minerals as well as being high in fibre and generally low in fat – all good ingredients for a healthy diet. Salad meals need not be time-consuming to prepare, nor restricted to summer months as there are ingredients that can be used all year round.

At the end of this chapter I've given a list of possible salad ingredients with a few notes on how to prepare them. Choose one or two ingredients from a section and put them with an appropriate dressing. If at first you feel a little unadventurous, start by thinking of a theme. A Mexican salad could contain avocado, peppers and tomatoes and have a spicy dressing. An Oriental salad might contain beansprouts, plums or pineapple and have a ginger dressing. Once you have experimented you will find it easy to invent ideas according to what you have available. As for quantities, much will depend on what else is being served. For a light starter or side dish, you will need enough to fill four small bowls or plates. If it is for a main meal, make two or three times this quantity, probably with different salads, and then choose an accompaniment from the list that shows you which ingredients will add substance. There are also a few general guidelines, plus a list of ingredients from which to make dressings. I hope you'll find these tips useful, but just to start you off here are four very different salad ideas.

CHICK PEA SALAD WITH CUMIN

*T*inned pulses are easy to turn in quick satisfying salads. Remember, though, that they do have a floury texture which needs to be counterbalanced with sharp flavours. Fresh fruit is ideal.

SERVES 4

1 × 14 oz (400 g) tin of chick peas, drained
1 dessert apple, cored and diced
2 oz (50 g) currants
4 spring onions, trimmed and diced

For the dressing:
½ teaspoon cumin seeds
2 tablespoons olive oil
1 tablespoon cider vinegar
1 teaspoon concentrated apple juice
1 teaspoon shoyu

Prepare all the salad ingredients and mix them together.

Roast the cumin seeds for 30 seconds in the microwave or in a dry frying pan for 2–3 minutes. Then mix the roasted seeds with the rest of the dressing ingredients.

Toss the dressing into the salad and serve immediately.

CREAMY PASTA SALAD

*W*holewheat pasta is a quick-cooking ingredient that is ideal in hearty salads. Shells or spiral shapes can be used, and mixed with many different nuts, fruits or vegetables. I find a thick creamy dressing works well. Watercress and yoghurt puréed together have a good colour and a pleasant peppery flavour that complements the pasta.

SERVES 4

6 oz (175 g) wholewheat pasta
1 bunch watercress
½ pint (300 ml) natural yoghurt

1 large red pepper, de-seeded
*   and diced*
2 oz (50 g) walnut pieces
Salt and pepper

Bring a large pan of salted water to the boil, add the pasta and cook for 8–10 minutes or until just tender. Drain thoroughly and rinse well in cold water to prevent any further cooking and to cool the pasta as quickly as possible.

Trim the watercress and purée it with the yoghurt until the mixture is smooth. Mix the yoghurt dressing into the cooked pasta, then add the prepared red pepper and walnut pieces. Season to taste.

LEAFY SALAD WITH LEMON DRESSING

*T*his is a refreshing light salad that can be used with starters or as a garnish for main courses. Preparing salad leaves is not too time-consuming, and you can vary the ingredients according to what is readily available. However, you can often buy ready prepared mixtures of interesting salad leaves and then all you need to do is toss in the dressing. When you can't get fresh tarragon, use a tarragon-flavoured vinegar.

SERVES 4

1 head of endive
1 small head of radicchio
2 oz (50 g) alfalfa sprouts
1 avocado, peeled and diced
1 punnet salad cress

For the dressing:
2 tablespoons olive oil
1 tablespoon white wine
   vinegar
Juice of ½ lemon
1 clove garlic, crushed
2 teaspoons fresh tarragon,
   chopped
Salt and pepper

Prepare the endive and radicchio by separating the leaves and wiping with a damp cloth if necessary. Mix these with the remaining ingredients.

Mix all the dressing ingredients together. Season well, and toss into the salad. Serve immediately.

MINIATURE VEGETABLE SALAD

*M*iniature and baby vegetables need little more preparation than washing, and are small enough to leave whole. In addition to those I've mentioned, you can add mangetout, mini avocados, or sugar snap peas. Chunky salads such as this go well with a creamy dressing. Poppy seeds add an interesting texture and flavour.

SERVES 4

4 oz (125 g) button mushrooms, wiped
4 oz (125 g) baby carrots, topped and washed
4 oz (125 g) baby sweetcorn, trimmed and roughly chopped
4 oz (125 g) cherry tomatoes

For the dressing:
2 tablespoons mayonnaise
2 tablespoons natural yoghurt
2 teaspoons grain mustard
4 teaspoons blue poppy seeds
1 clove garlic, crushed
Salt and pepper

Prepare the salad ingredients and mix them together in a large bowl.

Mix the dressing ingredients together and season well. Mix the dressing into the salad and serve straight away.

General Guidelines

* Be selective about what goes into a salad. It is better to make two bowls, with fewer ingredients in each, to give variety.
* Do not chop everything identically. Chunky pieces can be contrasted with finer shreds.
* Dress green, leafy salads at the last minute.
* Strongly flavoured ingredients are best chopped quite finely so they can be mixed in easily.
* Look out for ready prepared leaf salads. These are expensive but will save time. Also varieties of baby vegetables such as sweetcorn, parsnips, tomatoes and mushrooms. Again these need virtually no preparation.

Quick-to-prepare Ingredients

This list is by no means exhaustive but will give you some ideas on the easiest ingredients to prepare.

Leaves
Iceberg lettuce
Chinese leaves
Chicory
Radicchio
Cos lettuce

Notes on preparation: it is unnecessary to wash these tightly packed leaves. Don't chop them or they soon become limp: either leave them whole or tear into pieces.

Root Vegetables
Carrots
White radish or Mooli
Fennel

Notes on preparation: use the food processor to grate these.

Stalks and Stems
White and red cabbage
Celery

Notes on preparation: use the shredding blade of a food processor to prepare cabbage. Celery can be cut into chunks; use the leaves as well.

Vegetable Fruits
Avocado
Courgettes
Peppers
Tomatoes
Cucumber

Notes on preparation: apart from the avocado, these vegetable fruits only need to be washed and then cut in a number of ways, slice, dice, matchsticks or strips.

Pulses
Broad beans
Runner beans
French beans

Notes on preparation: these can be lightly cooked or, if very young, served raw. They are good mixed with other pulses such as cooked red kidney beans.

Fruits
Apple
Peach
Pineapple
Plum
Orange
Dates
Banana

Miscellaneous
Mushrooms (button)
Dried fruit
Olives
Capers
Herbs and spices
Tinned or frozen sweetcorn
Poppy and sesame seeds

INGREDIENTS WHICH ADD SUBSTANCE AND PROTEIN

Cooked grains such as rice, wheat or barley in a light vinaigrette
Cooked pasta tossed in mayonnaise or yoghurt
Bulgar wheat soaked in boiling water and dressed with lemon and olive oil
Varieties of tinned beans
Firm tofu, plain or marinated; silken tofu blended as a dressing
Chopped nuts
Grated cheese
Feta cheese
Beansprouts
Garlic bread or croûtons
Pitta bread
Hard-boiled egg

INGREDIENTS FOR SALAD DRESSINGS

Olive oil
Sunflower oil
Special oils such as walnut or hazelnut
Vinegars, wine or cider
Shoyu
Mayonnaise
Sour cream
Silken tofu
Yoghurt
Peanut butter or tahini
Fruit juices
Herbs and spices, including garlic and root ginger

BASIC VINAIGRETTE DRESSING

*T*here are plenty of good dressings to buy which enliven any salad, but it is easy to make your own and, once made, a vinaigrette mixture will keep several days in a cool place.

MAKES ¼ pint (150 ml)

5 tablespoons oil (either olive, sunflower or a mixture)
1–2 tablespoons wine or cider vinegar

2 teaspoons honey
1 teaspoon mustard
1 clove garlic, crushed

Mix all the ingredients together in a screw-top jar and shake well.

Variation: Tahini Dressing
Adding tahini to a vinaigrette makes the dressing creamy and nutty in flavour. Add more if you want the consistency of mayonnaise.

4 teaspoons tahini
2 teaspoons shoyu

Add these two ingredients to the basic vinaigrette and shake the jar vigorously.

Variation: Cottage Cheese and Apple Dressing

These ingredients thicken a basic vinaigrette to a mayonnaise consistency but also keep it light. This is a useful dressing for coleslaws, and waldorf salads.

8 oz (225 g) cottage cheese
1 tablespoon concentrated apple juice

Using a blender or liquidiser, mix these ingredients into the vinaigrette and blend until very smooth.

SPEEDY STIR-FRIES

*T*his is a very quick method of cooking vegetables and certain other ingredients. As the technique developed in the East, many people are under the illusion that stir-frying can only be used for Oriental-style dishes. This is not the case: virtually any mixture can be stir-fried. You can serve a stir-fry on its own, finish it off in a sauce, mix it with grated cheese, or add tofu, nuts and seeds for extra protein. Stir-fries can be served with rice or noodles, other types of pasta and grains, or baked potatoes.

The traditional cooking vessel is a wok which is in effect a large, rounded-based frying pan made of thin metal. It is useful for stir-frying as it heats quickly and gives a generous surface area for cooking, but a large frying pan does work fairly well.

QUICK TIPS

* Prepare all the vegetables before you start.
* Chop them into similar sized pieces so they cook evenly.
* Assemble any other ingredients you will need.
* Once the oil is initially flavoured with garlic and spices, keep the heat high to cook the vegetables as quickly as possible, so you get a good flavour and crisp texture.
* Have the rest of the meal ready so the stir-fry can be served immediately.

PEPPER AND ORANGE STIR-FRY

*T*his is a delicious colourful dish made with vegetables and other ingredients that need very little preparation as that often seems to be a disheartening factor with stir-fries. Served with rice or noodles, this makes a complete meal as there is some protein from the walnuts. Otherwise use it as an accompaniment to a baked dish or a roast, or as a pancake filling. It is not suitable for freezing.

SERVES 4

1 oz (25 g) walnuts, roughly chopped
2 teaspoons sunflower oil
1 clove garlic, crushed
2 peppers, de-seeded and diced
4 medium courgettes, wiped and sliced
8 oz (225 g) button mushrooms, wiped
1 orange, segmented

For the sauce:
Juice of 1 orange
1 tablespoon sunflower or walnut oil
1 teaspoon honey
1 teaspoon cumin seed
½ teaspoon arrowroot
Black pepper
1 bunch watercress

Lightly toast the walnut pieces for 1 minute in the microwave or for 2–3 minutes under the grill, turning them over to avoid burning.

Heat the oil in a wok or large frying pan and add the garlic. Fry briskly for a few seconds, then add the peppers and courgettes. Cook for 2 minutes, then add the mushrooms and cook for 3 minutes, stirring frequently. Add the orange pieces and toasted walnuts and stir in. Cook for 1 minute.

Mix the sauce ingredients together thoroughly, then pour into the pan. Stir well and cook until the sauce thickens slightly and the vegetables become a little tender. If you prefer them fairly well cooked, put a lid over the pan for a couple of minutes. Season to taste, then add the watercress and cook until the leaves wilt slightly. Serve immediately.

TOFU AND VEGETABLE STIR-FRY

Adding tofu to a stir-fry of vegetables makes a meal which is high in protein yet light. It is essential to have everything ready before you start cooking. Preparation time will depend on the number of ingredients used. The actual cooking time, though, is very short. Although it involves a little extra work, in this recipe it is best to fry the tofu first as this greatly improves the flavour. This stir-fry could be served with rice or noodles but should be eaten immediately it is cooked.

SERVES 4

For the sauce:
10 fl oz (300 ml) vegetable
   stock
2 tablespoons shoyu
1 tablespoon sherry
1 teaspoon sugar
1 teaspoon sesame oil
1 clove garlic, crushed
2 teaspoons root ginger, grated
1 teaspoon arrowroot

For the stir-fry:
10 oz (275 g) firm tofu
Sunflower oil for frying
1 clove garlic, crushed
6 oz (175 g) baby sweetcorn
1 medium fennel bulb, diced
1 large red pepper, de-seeded
   and sliced into strips
8 oz (225 g) broccoli florets
3 medium carrots, grated

Mix all the sauce ingredients together thoroughly.

For the stir-fry, chop the tofu into bite-sized pieces and prepare all the vegetables.

Heat 1 tablespoon oil in a wok or large frying pan, and briskly fry the garlic for a few seconds. Add the pieces of tofu, fry until slightly browned and remove from the pan. Heat 2 teaspoons of oil. Add the sweetcorn, stir in and cook for 1 minute. Add the fennel and continue frying and stirring for another minute, then add the red pepper and cook for 3 minutes. Add the broccoli and the fried tofu and cook for 2–3 minutes, stirring well. Pour over the sauce and mix well. Bring the mixture to the boil, add the carrot and simmer the sauce for 2–3 minutes or until it thickens and the vegetables are quite soft. Serve immediately.

SPINACH, PINE KERNEL AND SULTANA STIR-FRY

Spinach is not a vegetable that everybody likes, and I feel that often it is the texture that is off-putting. When it is stir-fried, however, it remains quite crisp. The pine kernels add a good texture and the sweetness of the sultanas complements the strong flavours. This dish makes a good hot starter, or a vegetable accompaniment to a bake or burger. It doesn't keep well, so make it and eat it straight away.

SERVES 4

1 tablespoon olive oil
2 lb (900 g) spinach, washed
    and shredded
2 cloves garlic, crushed

½ teaspoon grated nutmeg
2 oz (50 g) pine kernels
2 oz (50 g) sultanas
1 tablespoon lemon juice
Salt and black pepper

Heat the oil in a large pan and stir-fry the spinach in handfuls until it is all in the pan. Add the remaining ingredients and stir well. Cover the pan and cook for about 5 minutes or until the spinach is just tender. Season to taste. Serve hot with pitta bread as a starter or use as an accompaniment to a main dish.

HARVEST VEGETABLES WITH PARSLEY SAUCE

Stir-fries need not be made exclusively with Oriental ingredients. This recipe could be described as an English stir-fry, as the vegetables are cooked briefly using that method and then finished off covered and cooking in their own steam. To make it more than just a side vegetable, I add a quick parsley sauce, made using the blender. If you wish, you can top with seeds before serving, or with cheese and grill briefly. Any leftovers can be blended to make a tasty cream of vegetable soup!

SERVES 4

1 tablespoon sunflower oil	For the sauce:
2 leeks, cleaned and diced	1 oz (25 g) wholemeal flour
8 oz (225 g) carrots, scrubbed and chopped	1 oz (25 g) butter or sunflower margarine
8 oz (225 g) turnip or swede, peeled and chopped	1 pint (600 ml) milk
8 oz (225 g) Brussels sprouts, cleaned and halved	2 tablespoons parsley, roughly chopped
	Salt and black pepper

Heat the oil and fry the leeks for 3 minutes. Add the other vegetables, stir in well and, keeping the heat quite high, cook for 5 minutes. Reduce the heat, cover the pan and cook for 5–7 minutes or until the vegetables are just soft. If you find they are a little under-cooked for your taste, add a little water to the pan and cook for longer.

You could also cook these vegetables in the microwave: heat the oil for 30 seconds, then add the leeks and cook for 1 minute; add the remaining vegetables, cover the dish and cook for 6–8 minutes.

To prepare the sauce, blend all the ingredients together thoroughly for 1 minute. Pour into a pan and gradually bring to boiling point, stirring all the time. Simmer for 2–3 minutes. Season to taste. Put the cooked vegetables into a dish and pour over the sauce. If you wish, cover the mixture with seeds or grated cheese and grill for 2–3 minutes. Serve with a baked potato, or a cooked grain such as barley or millet.

ONE-POT RECIPES

A tasty sauce is an easy short cut to making a meal and can be made with very little preparation. Sauces can be cooked quickly in one pan, but even recipes that need slow simmering require very little attention. A pressure cooker can be used to cut down on the cooking time of some sauces, and I've included some basic notes about this invaluable gadget before the recipe section.

This chapter is divided into two sections. First there are five recipes that are designed to be served with pasta or noodles, or cooked grains such as rice or bulgar wheat. They could form a complete meal but would benefit from some accompaniment such as a side vegetable or salad, Parmesan or grated cheese, marinated tofu or chopped nuts.

The basis of two of these sauces is tomatoes as they are so quick to use and certainly needn't give predictable results. In one recipe, I suggest you add a colourful mixture of vegetables and herbs to create a tasty sauce. The second recipe includes a few pine kernels which, when added to a mushroom and tomato mixture, give a most unusual flavour.

The second part of the chapter contains more sustaining sauces and casseroles. These include a range of more substantial ingredients and the end result makes a main course. There are chestnuts in the Winter Warmer casserole; a creamy almond sauce covering a colourful mixture of steamed beans; black-eyed beans in a spiced casserole with nuts and seeds; a rich bolognese with lentils and tofu; and a creamy Mushroom Stroganoff. All these can be served with pasta, grains or a baked potato. Choose what you think is most appropriate.

If you need to create your own casseroles from what is on hand don't forget to use a good stock, a cube or powder. A tin of tomatoes, puréed, and some tomato purée will enrich the mixture. Don't forget flavourings such as shoyu, tabasco or mushroom ketchup. Spend a little time sweating the vegetables with onion as this will improve the final flavour. Dried chestnuts or tins of beans are quick ways to add substance, and a handful of bulgar wheat thickens the texture of a thin mixture.

Generally, stews for four people need about 1½–2 lb (750–900 g) of vegetables. You will find that simple combinations work well and it is not necessary to have more than two or three different vegetables in a mixture; you can then use other vegetables in a side dish.

When you have time, try to make extra as stews and casseroles freeze and reheat well. Remember, when reheating you may have to add some more stock and you will find the texture is softer. Casseroles can be served in a number of different guises: try a covering of mashed potato, a savoury crumble topping (page 108) or cornmeal batter (page 107).

QUICK TIPS

* Buy cartons of ready-chopped tomatoes to save you the job of blending.
* A little fresh parsley brings out the flavour of any dried herb used.
* A spoonful of shoyu or miso mixed in to a sauce or casserole will add a rich taste, especially if there hasn't been much time for the flavours to develop.
* For a very simple dressing, toss a little garlic or herbs with some butter or olive oil in to freshly cooked pasta. Be generous with the Parmesan.
* Most sauces and casseroles benefit from being made in advance and reheated.
* Try to make extra quantities when you have time, as sauces and casseroles freeze and reheat well.
* Yoghurt, cream or cream cheese mixed together or added singly make quick rich sauces.
* The easiest way to infuse milk for a plain well-flavoured white sauce is in the microwave.
* Purées of vegetables such as carrots make quick and useful sauces.
* Keep in stock a variety of stock cubes and mixes, sugar-free ketchups, relishes and chutneys.

THE PRESSURE COOKER

The pressure cooker is an invaluable time-saving gadget which can be used for cooking both individual ingredients as well as all-in-one meals such as casseroles and stews. Some people are worried by the inevitable hissing of steam that accompanies pressure cooking, but they are safe, providing you follow certain rules. As with all gadgets, the more you use them, the more familiar they become and invaluable they seem. The principle of pressure cooking is that when the atmospheric pressure is increased, the temperature at which liquids boil is raised accordingly and foods cook more quickly. The steam from a pressure cooker is released at a controlled rate, increasing the pressure and raising the temperature. The steam is forced through the food, both cooking and tenderising it.

How to use a pressure cooker

* The cooker must contain at least 10 fl oz (300 ml) liquid – i.e. water, stock, milk or wine.
* Make sure the lid is put on correctly: the lid handle should line up with the base handle.
* Put the correct weight on the centre vent and press it down until it clicks firmly into place. Some pressure cookers now have built-in weights. If you have a model like this, follow the manufacturer's instructions.
* Set the timer to the required cooking time. (Some pressure cookers can be set to reduce the pressure automatically, but you should follow the manufacturer's instructions.)
* Put the pressure cooker on to a high heat and wait for a steady hissing sound and flow of steam escaping from around the weights.
* Lower the heat so there is only a gentle hissing noise and an occasional escape of steam.
* At the end of the cooking period, move the pan away from the heat and allow 10–15 minutes for the pressure to reduce. Alternatively, immerse the pan in a sink full of cold water which will reduce the pressure in a matter of 2–3 minutes. If you have used the special setting on the automatic pressure cooker, the pressure will reduce very quickly. Do not remove the weight until the pressure has reduced.
* Once the weight is removed, the lid can be taken off and the contents checked for seasoning. You may find it is unnecessary to reheat the contents before serving.

Safety tips

* The cooker must never be more than *half* full with a soup or stew, and no more than *two-thirds* full with solid foods such as vegetables.
* Always use oven gloves to remove the weight.

Opposite: Pepper and Orange Stir-fry (page 59) and Spinach, Pine Kernel and Sultana Stir-fry (page 61)
Overleaf: Layered Cheesy Vegetables (page 41) and Red Cabbage Casserole (page 43)

COOKING GUIDELINES

Pulses

* Remember that pulses swell considerably during cooking, so it is best if the pan is not quite half full.
* Use 2 pints (1.2 litres) of liquid for every 1 lb (450 g) dry weight pulses.
* Bring to the boil and simmer gently; then cover, add the weight and bring to pressure.
* As a rough guide, pulses take one third of the time they would if cooked in an ordinary pan. For example, red kidney beans normally take 45–50 minutes. Cook them for 15 minutes in a pressure cooker.
* Pulses cooked at pressure are automatically fast-boiled for the whole of their cooking time, so any toxins will be destroyed.

Grains

* Like pulses, grains swell considerably during cooking, so have the pan no more than half full.
* With barley and wheat, use 1½ pints (900 ml) of liquid for every 4 oz (125 g) dry weight. Cook for 20 minutes.
* With rice, use 1¼ pints (750 ml) of liquid for every 4 oz (125 g) dry weight. Cook for 8 minutes.

Dried fruit

* Soak the fruit for about 10 minutes first in boiling water, using 1 pint (600 ml) water to 1 lb (450 g) fruit.
* Cook the fruit in the soaking water.
* Apricots and peaches take roughly 3–5 minutes.
* Fruit salad mixtures need 10 minutes.

Casseroles, Stews and Soups

* Generally 10–20 minutes is enough to cook a stew thoroughly and draw out the flavours.

Overleaf: Creamed Red Lentil and Coconut Sauce (page 75); Black-eyed Bean Casserole (page 79); Creamy Almond Vegetables (page 78); and Broccoli and Blue Cheese Sauce (page 74)
Opposite: Mushroom and Cheese Croustade (page 87) and Sweetcorn Loaf (page 92) with tomato sauce

PINE KERNEL AND TOMATO SAUCE

*P*ine kernels have a distinctive flavour and are a splendid addition to sauces which would otherwise be rather ordinary. Apart from adding flavour they are also a good source of protein. Although they are an expensive ingredient, only a few are needed to make a difference.

SERVES 4

1 tablespoon olive oil
1 onion, peeled and finely chopped
1 clove garlic, crushed
8 oz (225 g) button mushrooms, wiped and halved
1 × 14 oz (400 g) tin of tomatoes
1 red pepper, de-seeded and chopped
2 tablespoons parsley, roughly chopped
1 teaspoon dried oregano
1 oz (25 g) pine kernels
Salt and black pepper

Heat the oil and gently fry the onion for 3 minutes. Add the garlic and mushrooms and cook for a further 3 minutes. Using a blender, purée the tomatoes with the red pepper and parsley until smooth. Pour this mixture into the pan and add the oregano. Bring to the boil, add the pine kernels, cover the pan and simmer for 30 minutes. (Or pressure cook for 10.) Season to taste. Serve hot.

SIMPLE VEGETABLE SAUCE

*T*his type of sauce, of which I make many variations according to what is in season or in the larder, is almost more of a casserole as it is chunky in texture and definitely needs to be eaten with a fork rather than a spoon. It goes well with virtually any grain, either one which you have cooked simply or a more complex recipe such as the Nice Spice Rice (page 28). Try to choose a good mix of vegetables so that you get a variety of colour, texture and flavour. To make the meal more substantial, you could add some grated cheese or make a quick tofu dish. This sauce will freeze but some of the texture is lost. In that case you may prefer to blend it and turn it into soup.

SERVES 4

1 tablespoon olive oil
1 onion, peeled and finely chopped
1 clove garlic, crushed
1 lb (450 g) mixed vegetables (carrots, courgettes, mushrooms and cabbage), cut into large chunks

1 × 14 oz (400 g) tin of tomatoes, puréed
1 tablespoon tomato purée
2 tablespoons parsley, finely chopped
1 teaspoon dried oregano
Shoyu to taste
Salt and black pepper

Heat the oil and gently fry the onion for 3 minutes, then add the garlic and cook for 1 minute. Add the vegetables to the pan. Cook gently for 5 minutes, stirring well. Stir in the tomatoes, tomato purée and herbs, and simmer for 35–40 minutes. If you are using a pressure cooker, bring to pressure and cook for 10 minutes. Add the shoyu and season to taste. Serve hot with grains, pasta or baked potatoes.

BROCCOLI AND BLUE CHEESE SAUCE

*T*his rich and colourful mixture makes a quick sauce to serve with pasta. As it is quite chunky in texture, choose a complementary pasta shape such as a shell or spiral. The robust flavours of blue cheese and broccoli also work well with buckwheat. This sauce will not freeze.

SERVES 4

8 oz (225 g) broccoli florets

For the sauce:
1 oz (25 g) butter or margarine
6 oz (175 g) blue cheese
4–5 fl oz (125–150 ml) milk
2 teaspoons cider vinegar
Salt and black pepper

Steam the broccoli florets for 8–10 minutes, or cook them on full power in a microwave for 6 minutes. (To cook in a microwave, place the florets in a large dish, add 2–3 tablespoons water, then cover the dish. Half-way through the cooking, stir the florets or re-arrange them.)

Meanwhile make the sauce. Melt the butter over a gentle heat, then crumble in the cheese and let it melt slowly. Add the milk and beat in well. Stir in the cider vinegar and season carefully as blue cheese is quite salty.

Pour the sauce over the freshly cooked broccoli and serve immediately with pasta, noodles or buckwheat.

CREAMED RED LENTIL AND COCONUT SAUCE

*C*reamed coconut has a marvellous velvet-like quality and it certainly lifts the otherwise earthy flavour of the lentils. Store creamed coconut in the refrigerator, as it has a high fat content and may go rancid in warm temperatures. This recipe is a cross between a sauce and a dip or dhal. You can adjust the liquid content to complement the rest of the meal.

SERVES 4

1 tablespoon sunflower oil
1 onion, peeled and finely chopped
1 clove garlic, crushed
½ teaspoon turmeric
1 teaspoon garam masala
8 oz (225 g) red lentils
1 pint (600 ml) boiling vegetable stock or water
1–2 oz (25–50 g) creamed coconut, grated
Salt and black pepper

Heat the oil and gently fry the onion for 3 minutes. Mix the spices with a little water, stir in to the onion, add the garlic and cook for 2 minutes. Then stir in the lentils, fry for 1 minute and pour over the boiling stock or water. Bring to the boil, then cover the pan and cook the lentils over a gentle heat for 20 minutes or until quite soft. Dissolve the grated coconut in a little boiling water and stir it into the cooked lentils. The resulting mixture should be quite soft but not sloppy. Season to taste. Serve this dish warm with rice or bread.

Peanut and Sesame Sauce

*P*eanut butter and sesame paste, or tahini, can be used in a number of ways to make quick sauces or dressings. Both have strong flavours and rich textures, so you don't need to use much. They work well when flavoured with slightly acidic ingredients such as citrus or other fruit juices, or yoghurt; you could also try different hot spices, particularly ginger.

This sauce is a useful recipe if you are on your own as it can be made up in small quantities, and any leftovers will keep 2–3 days in the refrigerator. Use the sauce over grains or vegetables, or make it with less apple juice and serve it cold as a salad dressing.

SERVES 4

1 tablespoon peanut butter
1 tablespoon tahini or sesame
paste
1 small onion, finely chopped

1 teaspoon honey
Juice of ½ lemon
7–10 fl oz (200–300 ml) weak
apple juice
1–2 teaspoons shoyu

Blend all the ingredients together thoroughly so the sauce is smooth. Heat gently in a small pan, stirring constantly. The sauce will thicken a little as it cooks. Serve hot.

WINTER WARMER

*D*ried chestnuts will keep for at least a year in the store cupboard and they are an invaluable addition to casseroles and roasts. They can be cooked with other ingredients as in this recipe, but remember to add enough water as they expand considerably. If you wish to cook chestnuts on their own, they don't need to be soaked. Just bring them to the boil in plenty of water and then simmer until the nuts are cooked through – allow about 45–60 minutes in an ordinary pan or 15 minutes in a pressure cooker. The cooking stock is delicious and quite sweet. You can make this casserole with a number of different vegetables. I think the hearty flavour of kale works particularly well. This dish freezes well and can also be kept in the refrigerator for 3–4 days. Serve it with grains such as barley or jacket potatoes.

SERVES 4

1 tablespoon sunflower oil
1 onion, peeled and finely
  chopped
8 oz (225 g) leeks, cleaned and
  chopped
8 oz (225 g) swede, peeled and
  chopped
8 oz (225 g) kale or broccoli,
  roughly chopped

4 oz (125 g) dried chestnuts
1 teaspoon dried thyme
1 bay leaf
1 × 14 oz (400 g) tin of
  tomatoes, puréed
1 tablespoon tomato purée
10 fl oz (300 ml) onion stock
1 tablespoon shoyu
Salt and black pepper

Heat the oil and gently fry the onion for 3 minutes, then add the vegetables and stir in well. Cook for 5 minutes over a gentle heat, then add the remaining ingredients and simmer for 45–60 minutes. (If you are using a pressure cooker, bring the mixture up to pressure and cook for 15 minutes.) Leave to cool, then season to taste. Reheat if necessary before serving.

CREAMY ALMOND VEGETABLES

*N*ut sauces, particularly ones made from almonds or cashews, are very creamy and add an almost instant flavour to any steamed vegetable mixture. Make sure the sauce is well seasoned as, although nuts are a rich ingredient, they can be a little bland once cooked. This dish does not freeze or keep very well.

SERVES 4

8 oz (225 g) leeks, cleaned and chopped
8 oz (225 g) French beans, frozen or fresh
8 oz (225 g) cauliflower florets

For the sauce:
3 oz (75 g) ground almonds
10 fl oz (300 ml) stock
2 tablespoons parsley, chopped
1 teaspoon horseradish
1 bay leaf
Salt and black pepper

2 oz (50 g) flaked almonds

Prepare all the vegetables and either steam or microwave for 8–10 minutes or until just tender.

Meanwhile prepare the sauce. Blend the ground almonds with the stock, parsley and horseradish. Pour the sauce into a small pan, add the bay leaf and bring the sauce to the boil, stirring continually. Cook for 2–3 minutes so that it thickens, then season well. Remove the bay leaf.

Put the steamed vegetables into an ovenproof dish and pour over the sauce. Cover with flaked almonds and grill for 2–3 minutes to brown them slightly. Serve hot.

BLACK-EYED BEAN CASSEROLE

*B*lack-eyed beans are one of the quickest-cooking of the larger pulses. Beans generally need to be soaked for several hours before cooking, as this gives them a chance to rehydrate properly and to release some indigestible starches. With black-eyed beans, however, you can leave out this stage when you are in a hurry. Other beans which needn't necessarily be soaked are aduki, mung and flageolet.

You could make this recipe even more quickly using tinned beans – either black-eyed, red kidney, ful mesdames or whole lentils.

SERVES 4

8 oz (225 g) black-eyed beans
1 tablespoon olive oil
1 onion, peeled and finely
  chopped
2 sticks celery, diced
1 green pepper, de-seeded and
  diced
1 teaspoon paprika
½ teaspoon ground cumin
½ teaspoon ground cinnamon
¼ teaspoon chilli powder
2 oz (50 g) sunflower seeds
2 oz (50 g) raisins or currants
1 × 14 oz (400 g) tin of
  tomatoes, puréed
1 tablespoon shoyu
10 fl oz (300 ml) vegetable
  stock
Salt and black pepper

Rinse the beans thoroughly and cover with water. Bring up to pressure, then cook for 15 minutes. (You can, of course, make this recipe without using a pressure cooker – simply bring the pan to the boil and simmer the beans for 45 minutes.) Leave to cool and then drain, reserving the stock.

While the beans are cooking, prepare the vegetables and assemble the remaining ingredients.

Using the pressure cooker again, heat the oil and gently fry the onion and celery for 3 minutes, add the pepper and spices and cook for 2 minutes, then add the cooked beans, sunflower seeds, raisins, tomatoes, and shoyu. Add enough stock so the casserole is moist, then bring the mixture to pressure and cook for 15 minutes. (If you are using an ordinary pan, cook for 45 minutes.) Leave to cool, then season well. Re-heat if necessary before serving.

LENTIL AND TOFU BOLOGNESE

*R*ed split lentils and brown whole lentils both make very good vegetarian versions of bolognese sauce as they have the right texture. Extra flavour comes from vegetables: mushrooms are ideal, but you could also use peppers or courgettes. I find that adding silken tofu makes the sauce a little more creamy and helps to bring all the flavours together. This sauce does not freeze well as the texture changes, but it can be kept in the refrigerator for 3–4 days and reheats well.

SERVES 4

1 tablespoon olive oil
1 onion, peeled and finely
    chopped
1 clove garlic, crushed
8 oz (225 g) field or flat
    mushrooms, sliced

4 oz (125 g) red lentils, cleaned
10 oz (275 g) silken tofu
2 tablespoons tomato purée
1 teaspoon dried oregano or
    marjoram
5 fl oz (150 ml) water
1–2 tablespoons shoyu
Salt and black pepper

Heat the oil and gently fry the onion for 3 minutes, then add the garlic and mushrooms and cook for 5 minutes. Add the lentils, mix in well and cook for 2 minutes, stirring frequently so they do not catch.

Blend the silken tofu with the tomato purée until smooth. Pour this over the lentil mixture, adding the water and herbs. Bring the sauce to the boil, then cover the pan and simmer gently for 25 minutes, stirring frequently. Add a little more water if necessary. The sauce is ready when the lentils are well softened. Add the shoyu and season to taste. Serve hot.

MUSHROOM STROGANOFF

*T*his is a quickly made delicious dish that can be easily scaled down to serve one or two people. Serve with freshly cooked pasta, rice or a jacket potato and perhaps a side salad of mixed leaves. Because of the mixed cream dressing, it will not freeze.

SERVES 4

1 tablespoon olive oil
1 lb (450 g) leeks, sliced
1 lb (450 g) mushrooms,
    quartered
1 clove garlic, crushed

1 teaspoon paprika
1 teaspoon wholemeal flour
6 fl oz (175 ml) crème fraîche
5 fl oz (150 ml) soured cream
1 teaspoon shoyu
Salt and black pepper

Heat the oil and gently fry the leeks for 5 minutes, then add the mushrooms, garlic and paprika and continue cooking for 10 minutes, stirring occasionally. Don't cover the pan or else you will create too much liquid which will make the stroganoff watery. Stir in the flour and cook for 1 minute.

In a small bowl, mix together the crème fraîche and soured cream, then add this and the shoyu to the cooked mushroom mixture. Cook the sauce over a low heat just long enough to heat through. Season to taste.

TIME-SAVING GADGETS

*T*here's no doubt that gadgets such as blenders and food processors have revolutionised many aspects of cooking. Gone are the days when smooth soups could only be achieved with endless sieving, and grinding nuts or grating breadcrumbs were laborious chores. In this chapter I have concentrated specifically on recipes that use food processing techniques to some extent, although you will have noticed that these techniques are widely used through the rest of the book as well, as they do save time. A few notes about food processors and similar gadgets are just before the recipe section. Of course, you will still be able to make all these recipes even without 'hi-tech' equipment – it will just take slightly longer.

The recipes in this chapter are all savoury main courses. There are two delicious flans, with quickly made crumb crusts which give the quiches a real bite. This saves you the worry of making pastry and the task of rolling it out.

I've included a basic nut roast as it is such a popular and versatile recipe, as well as some nut and vegetable burgers, and a nut crumble equally successful with adults and children.

There is a grain and vegetable loaf which is good hot or cold, and an easy savoury, made with a vegetable purée, for a warming supper dish. Finally I've included some potato pancakes, made with a blended batter, that make a quick snack meal for one or two, or could be used to accompany another main course.

There are a number of different gadgets for grating, grinding, slicing or puréeing ingredients; if you want to save time and effort when cooking, a piece of equipment such as this is invaluable. To get the maximum benefit, however, any machine of this type should be kept ready for use on a convenient work surface. Below, I've briefly described the different functions of the various pieces of equipment available. This will give you some idea of what to look for if you are buying for the first time or replacing out-of-date machines.

BLENDER

Functions:
* Capable of blending liquids such as soups and sauces to a very smooth texture.
* Capable of grinding dry ingredients such as nuts or bread-crumbs, but only in fairly small quantities.

Things to look out for:
* Goblets with a removable base and blades are much easier to clean.
* Best results are obtained at high speed, so check on the power of the motor.
* A pulsing facility, which allows quick on/off bursts, is useful for controlling the texture, but not essential.
* Buy a blender with a large capacity – eg 2 pints (1.2 litres) – so you can process quite substantial amounts of liquid in one go.

FOOD PROCESSOR

Functions:
* Can shred, chop, slice, grind, grate and purée.
* Capable of blending liquids for soups, but doesn't give as smooth a result as a separate blender goblet.

Useful Attachments:
* Steel blade, which is razor sharp for chopping vegetables and herbs, grinding nuts and making breadcrumbs, puréeing fruit, rubbing in fat for pastry.
* Fine and coarse slicing plates for vegetables and fruit.
* Fine and coarse shredding plates for cheese, vegetables and fruit.
* Whisk for egg white, whisked sponge and cream. This may not give as good a result as a separate whisk and bowl.
* Extra attachments are dough hook, plastic blade, spice mill, and chipping blade.

Things to look out for:
* High-powered machines, as these produce better results.
* A good seal so that liquid does not leak when you are blending a soup for example.
* A machine with a separate blender goblet.

MIXER WITH ATTACHMENTS

Functions:
* A simple mixer is very efficient for whisking and beating operations. It usually consists of a bowl with beaters, whisk and dough hook.
* With extra attachments this machine has all the facilities of the food processor.

Things to look out for:
* Check you have room to keep this machine handy. It is more cumbersome than a food processor, and it takes more time to switch attachments.

QUICK TIPS

* Try to organise your work so that the dry ingredients are processed before the wet, as this avoids washing-up.
* Process larger amounts of items such as breadcrumbs and nuts – these can then be frozen in useful quantities.
* Process foods of similar texture together – for example, root vegetables, or soft vegetables like mushrooms or tomatoes.
* A purée of onion with garlic and spices makes a quick basic flavouring for a savoury dish.
* When preparing vegetables that are to be cooked and puréed, grate them first as this will speed up their cooking time.
* Fresh herbs, especially parsley, can be processed in small batches, then stored in the refrigerator or frozen.
* Dried fruit need be only just soft before it can be puréed.
* Purée left-over vegetables to make quick sauces.
* It is not always necessary to purée the whole of a soup. Leave some pieces still in chunks to give a different texture.
* Don't over-process flour mixtures when making cakes or they become heavy.

MUSHROOM AND CHEESE CROUSTADE

*T*his dish is rather like a quiche but with certainly enough crunch to appeal to real men! The crust is an easily prepared mixture of bread-crumbs, flakes and flour bound together with melted butter (or margarine) and then baked briefly before being filled. It is a good alternative to pastry and, if you still haven't quite perfected the art of making wholemeal pastry, a great deal easier.

Mushrooms make a marvellous filling as they need little prepar-ation, but you could use a number of other vegetables instead. This quiche will freeze, in which case it is better served slightly warm.

SERVES 4

For the crust:
4 oz (125 g) wholemeal
    breadcrumbs
1 oz (25 g) wholemeal flour
1 oz (25 g) wheatgerm
2 oz (50 g) oatmeal
1/2 teaspoon salt
1 teaspoon dried marjoram
4 oz (125 g) butter

For the filling:
1 tablespoon sunflower oil
1 onion, peeled and finely
    chopped
8 oz (225 g) mushrooms, wiped
    and diced
4 oz (125 g) Cheddar cheese,
    grated
2 eggs
5 fl oz (150 ml) milk
Salt and black pepper

Pre-heat the oven to gas mark 6, 400°F (200°C).

Mix together the breadcrumbs, flour, wheatgerm, oatmeal, salt and herbs in a large bowl. Melt the butter, pour it over the dry ingredients and mix in well. Press the crumb dough into a greased 8 in. (20 cm) flan case. Bake for 10 minutes. Leave to cool.

Meanwhile prepare the filling. Heat the oil and gently fry the onion for 3 minutes, then add the mushrooms and cook for 5 minutes or until they are just soft. Remove the pan from the heat. Cover the crumb case with the grated cheese, then spoon over the mushrooms. Beat the eggs and milk together, season well and pour over the top. Bake for 35 minutes or until the filling is just set. Serve with hot vegetables or a salad.

CURRIED BEAN CROUSTADE

*T*his croustade is a variation on the previous recipe, adding peanuts to the base to give a slightly different flavour. The filling uses tinned beans, which are ideal as they tend on the whole to be soft. They are also quite salty and so prevent the mixture from being bland – but remember to take this into account when you add seasoning yourself.

SERVES 4

For the crust:
4 oz (125 g) wholemeal
   breadcrumbs
1 oz (25 g) wholemeal flour
1 oz (25 g) peanuts, ground
2 oz (50 g) oatmeal
½ teaspoon salt
1 teaspoon dried marjoram
4 oz (125 g) butter

For the filling:
5 fl oz (150 ml) milk
2 eggs
2 tablespoons parsley, roughly
   chopped
1 teaspoon stock powder
½–1 teaspoon curry powder
1 × 14 oz (400 g) tin of butter
   or cannelini beans, drained
Salt and black pepper

Pre-heat the oven to gas mark 6, 400°F (200°C).

    Mix together the breadcrumbs, flour, peanuts, oatmeal, salt and herbs in a large bowl. Melt the butter in a small pan or in the microwave. Pour it over the dry ingredients and mix in well. Press the crumb dough into a greased 8 in. (20 cm) flan case. Bake for 10 minutes. Leave to cool.

    For the filling, blend the milk with the eggs, parsley, stock powder and curry powder. Then stir in the drained beans. Season to taste. Pour the filling into the crumb case and bake for 35 minutes or until just set. Serve hot or cold.

NUT 'N SEED ROAST

*T*his is a versatile nut roast mixture that can be baked in a conventional oven or in the microwave. Nut roasts are easy to prepare. The main point to remember is that the initial mixture should be moist as the nuts and oats will absorb quite an amount of liquid and it is essential that the roast does not dry out. Secondly, the mixture needs to be well seasoned or it will seem bland. This recipe has a tomato stock and a good spoonful of mustard. Extra texture in this roast comes from whole sunflower seeds, although you could try pine kernels as an alternative.

Nut roasts are filling, so serve them in small portions with a sauce or relish. This recipe freezes well, and will reheat in a microwave without drying out, but it is also tasty eaten cold.

SERVES 4

1 tablespoon olive oil
1 onion, peeled and finely chopped
2 sticks celery, diced
4 oz (125 g) nut pieces
1–2 oz (25–50 g) sunflower seeds
4 oz (125 g) medium oatmeal
1 × 7 oz (200 g) tin of tomatoes, puréed
1 tablespoon tomato purée
1 teaspoon dried thyme
1 teaspoon English mustard, prepared
Salt and black pepper

If you are using a conventional oven, pre-heat the oven to gas mark 5, 375°F (190°C).

Heat the oil and gently fry the onion and celery for 5 minutes or until quite soft.

In a separate bowl, mix together the remaining ingredients and stir in the cooked onion and celery. Season to taste. Check the mixture is fairly moist, adding a little stock or water if necessary. Spoon into a lightly greased dish and bake for 25 minutes. (If you want to use a microwave, choose a suitable dish and bake for 8–10 minutes on full power, or bake individual portions for 2½–3 minutes.)

Leave to stand for 2 minutes before serving, as this gives it time to firm up, making it easier to slice.

Parsnip and Hazel Burgers

*N*ut burgers, like nut roasts, need to be moist and well flavoured to be successful, but they are extremely simple to make. Vegetable purées can be used as the moistening agent. I have used parsnips in this version and they are quick to cook if you prepare them using the grating blade of the food processor. You could try other root vegetables instead.

Burgers can be served in a bun, and this does make a very satisfying supper. Otherwise serve them with a sauce, a stir-fry or steamed vegetables, and a potato or salad. The burgers will freeze, but in that case don't coat or fry them, merely shape the mixture ready for those stages.

MAKES 8 burgers

1 lb (450 g) parsnips, finely grated
1 tablespoon olive oil
1 onion, peeled and finely chopped
2 teaspoons cumin seeds
4 oz (125 g) hazelnuts, coarsely ground

2 oz (50 g) breadcrumbs
1 egg yolk
Salt and black pepper

For the coating:
1 egg white
2 oz (50 g) breadcrumbs

Oil for frying

Put the grated parsnips in a pan with some boiling water and cook for 4 minutes or until just tender. Drain and set aside.

In a separate pan, heat the oil and gently cook the onion for 3 minutes, then add the cumin seeds and cook for 2 minutes to bring out the flavour of the spice. Mix the nuts thoroughly into the onion mixture.

In a large bowl, mix together the parsnips, onion and nut mixture and breadcrumbs. Stir very thoroughly and beat in the egg yolk. Season to taste. Shape the mixture into 8 burgers, then coat in egg white and breadcrumbs.

Shallow-fry the burgers for 4 minutes on each side so they are heated right through and well browned.

CRUNCHY CASHEW CASSEROLE

*N*uts are an ideal ingredient to add to a basic vegetable mixture for instant protein and extra texture. You should allow about 2 oz (50 g) per person: if you serve a much bigger quantity than this you may find it becomes too rich. It is important to have a well-flavoured stock in a recipe such as this and I find a shop-bought onion stock cube ideal. A yeast extract would be too strong. This dish has a quick crumble topping which makes it more of a complete meal. Serve with a plainly cooked vegetable or some pulses such as chick peas in a tomato sauce, and creamed or baked potatoes. However, if you wish to make just the sauce, add extra nuts, and serve it as a vegetable sauce with grains or pasta.

SERVES 4

For the sauce:
1 tablespoon sunflower oil
1 onion, peeled and finely
  chopped
3 oz (75 g) cashew pieces
12 oz (350 g) mixed vegetables
  (carrots, parsnips, sprouts),
  roughly chopped
8 oz (225 g) winter cabbage,
  finely shredded
1 oz (25 g) wholemeal flour

1 teaspoon rosemary
1 teaspoon sage
1 pint (600 ml) onion stock
1 tablespoon shoyu
Salt and black pepper

For the topping:
3 oz (75 g) cashew pieces,
  ground
1 oz (25 g) wholemeal flour
2 oz (50 g) medium oatmeal
2–3 tablespoons sunflower oil

Pre-heat the oven to gas mark 5, 375°F (190°C).

Heat the oil and gently fry the onion for 3 minutes. Add the cashew pieces and cook so they toast lightly. Add the vegetables to the pan and cook for 5 minutes. Next sprinkle over the flour and cook for 1 minute. Then add the herbs, stock and shoyu and bring to the boil. Simmer for 15 minutes. Season to taste.

Meanwhile prepare the topping by mixing the ingredients together and rub in the oil.

Put the cooked sauce into a lightly oiled ovenproof dish and sprinkle over the topping. Bake for 20–25 minutes. Serve hot.

SWEETCORN LOAF

*T*he ingredients for this loaf can be easily prepared using a food processor; everything is then mixed together and bound with beaten egg. The resulting light-coloured loaf is delicately flavoured but quite substantial. It makes a good cold meal with salads, but could also be served hot with a mushroom or tomato sauce.

SERVES 4

1 small onion, chopped
1 carrot, grated
1 apple, cored and grated
4 oz (125 g) cashew pieces, ground
2 oz (50 g) wholemeal breadcrumbs

2 oz (50 g) porridge oats
1 × 7 oz (200 g) tin sweetcorn, drained
2 teaspoons mixed herbs
2 eggs, beaten
1 tablespoon shoyu
1 teaspoon bouillon powder
Salt and black pepper

Pre-heat the oven to gas mark 6, 400°F (200°C).

Mix all the ingredients in a large bowl; the mixture should be quite moist. Season to taste. Spoon into a lightly greased ovenproof dish and bake for 40 minutes or until quite firm. Alternatively, cook in the microwave at full power for 10–12 minutes and then leave to stand. Serve hot or cold.

CREAMED POTATO SAVOURY

A vegetable purée, mixed with cheese and then quickly grilled, makes a good simple supper. This recipe can be served with a contrasting steamed vegetable such as carrots and a light leafy salad mixture, or an interesting bread such as a rye loaf or pumpernickel. If you want a more substantial meal, make an omelette or a casserole as a complementary dish.

This recipe does not freeze and is really best made and eaten immediately.

SERVES 4

1 lb (450 g) potatoes, peeled and diced
8 oz (225 g) turnips, scrubbed and diced
1 lb (450 g) Brussels sprouts
1–2 oz (25–50 g) sunflower margarine

1 teaspoon dried sage
2 oz (50 g) Cheddar cheese, grated
Salt and black pepper
Sesame seeds or extra cheese for the topping

If you have a microwave put the potatoes and turnips in a large bowl, add 2–3 tablespoons water and cover. Microwave for 7 minutes, then add the sprouts and microwave the vegetables for another 5 minutes or until they are fairly soft. Allow for the fact that they will continue cooking after they are removed from the microwave.

Alternatively, steam or boil the vegetables for about 20 minutes or until soft. Drain well.

Once cooked, purée the vegetables until smooth in the food processor, adding the margarine, sage and cheese. Season to taste.

Spoon into an attractive dish and serve immediately, or sprinkle with sesame seeds or extra cheese and grill for 2–3 minutes.

POTATO PANCAKES

*T*his is a good meal to make for two. The actual preparation is very quick but you will have to spend a little time organising the cooking of the pancakes. As you finish each batch of pancakes, keep them warm in the oven, preferably covered to prevent them drying out.

These pancakes are popular in Germany served with apple sauce, and I think they go well with the Winter Warmer recipe (page 77) or the Red Cabbage Casserole (page 43). The pancakes do not freeze or keep well, so make them as they are needed.

MAKES 8–10 small cakes

2 eggs
2 fl oz (50 ml) milk
1 clove garlic, crushed
2 tablespoons parsley, chopped
8 oz (225 g) potato, scrubbed
   and chopped

1–2 oz (25–50 g) wholemeal
   self-raising flour
6–8 drops tabasco
Salt and black pepper
Oil or butter for frying

Blend the eggs, milk, garlic and parsley together for 30 seconds. Add ¾ of the potato and blend for 30 seconds, then add the flour and tabasco and blend for 30 seconds. Add the last of the potato and blend in roughly so the texture of the batter isn't entirely smooth, then season to taste.

Heat a large non-stick pan and using either butter or oil fry tablespoons of the mixture to make small pancakes. You can make 4–5 at a time and fry until they are well browned. Serve hot.

PAINLESS PUDDINGS

*A*s with the section on starters I've devised a few recipes to give you ideas for simple puddings and desserts that can be part of a total quick meal or save you time on any other occasion.

Dried fruits are useful and versatile ingredients from which a number of desserts can be created. They can be cooked with spices and served hot or cold as an alternative to fresh fruit salad. Alternatively, cook and purée them, and mix with cream, yoghurt, soft cheese or tofu to make a variety of whips and fools. If you want something slightly more elaborate, these can easily be layered with nuts, flakes or fresh fruit. I've given a couple of recipes covering these ideas.

Tofu has been mentioned already in connection with savoury recipes. Silken tofu is very useful for sweet dishes as it combines happily with most flavours and when blended has a good smooth texture. Because of its long shelf life, it has an advantage over dairy products as you can keep some in stock for emergencies. Once you have tried the two recipes included here, you'll see its potential.

As fresh fruit salad is such a popular dessert and suitable on so many occasions, I've included some tips for saving time in preparing fruit. There is also a simple baked apple dish with a very straightforward filling. Apart from the pudding mentioned here, there ars six more ideas in the Meals in Minutes section.

You'll find more notes on useful dairy products, tofu and dried fruit in the introduction to the book.

QUICK TIPS

* Mix honey with a thick-set yoghurt and sprinkle with chopped nuts.
* Serve a platter of unusual raw dried fruits and nuts in shells.
* Purée soft fruit such as strawberries, gooseberries or plums, and serve with ice cream.
* Mix soft fruit purées with crème fraîche or thick double cream for a rich fruit fool.
* A crisp granola-style cereal makes an instant crunchy topping for stewed fruit.
* Serve fresh fruit with an interesting cheese and make sure you have a good contrast of texture, such as a firm fruit with a soft cheese.

* Keep in stock fruit tinned in its own juices. Serve it with toasted nuts or seeds.
* Try unusual fresh fruits such as pomegranates or mango. These could be served by themselves.
* Liven up commonplace fruit by serving it with nut or seed toppings. Try fresh banana sprinkled with wheatgerm and sunflower seeds.
* Have good-quality ice creams and sorbets in the freezer for emergencies.

SPICED FRUIT COMPOTE

*T*his warming dessert takes virtually no time to prepare, and not long to cook either. Any leftovers can be reheated, or served cold either as another day's pudding, or for a special breakfast. It is very easy to make double quantities.

SERVES 4

8 oz (225 g) mixed dried fruit, soaked overnight
1 pint (600 ml) apple juice
1 stick cinnamon
1 bay leaf
4 allspice berries

Put the dried fruit mixture, apple juice and spices in a pan. Bring to the boil, then cover and simmer for 30–40 minutes. Add more apple juice or water if necessary. Remove the spices. Serve hot or cold with yoghurt or cream.

APRICOT WHIP

When cut into thin slivers, dried apricots will cook enough to purée in about 15–20 minutes, and about 10 minutes in a microwave. They are ideal for simple puddings as they have such a good flavour and colour. In this recipe, I have mixed them with whipped egg white to create a mousse-like texture, but for even more simple ideas, mix in thick double cream or a set yoghurt.

SERVES 4

8 oz (225 g) dried apricots
2 eggs, separated

4–6 tablespoons natural
  yoghurt or silken tofu
Honey to taste
A little brandy (optional)

Cut the apricots into thin slivers with a pair of scissors. Place in a pan of hot water, bring to the boil, cover and simmer for 15–20 minutes, or until just soft enough to purée. Alternatively, microwave for about 10 minutes. Drain and leave to cool slightly.

   Purée the apricots with the egg yolks and yoghurt or tofu until smooth.

   Whisk the egg whites until stiff and fold into the purée, adding the honey and brandy to taste. Spoon into glasses or glass dishes.

TOFU AND SESAME CREAM

*S*ilken tofu makes a good basic ingredient for quick desserts. It can be kept for several months in the packet so it is always possible to have some on hand for emergencies. When taken out of the packet it does look rather solid, but once blended with other ingredients in a food processor or blender it turns into a delicious smooth cream. Tofu has little taste of its own but will absorb whatever flavours you put with it. The consistency can be thick or thin, depending on what you blend with it.

SERVES 4

10 oz (275 g) silken tofu
4 tablespoons tahini, or sesame paste
4 tablespoons orange juice
1 tablespoon honey
Juice of ½ lemon
1 oz (25 g) carob chocolate

Blend the tofu with the tahini, orange juice and honey. Then add the lemon juice to taste. Grate the carob chocolate and blend with the tofu mixture for a few seconds. Pour the tofu cream into attractive glasses. Decorate with extra grated carob if you wish.

FRUIT AMBROSIA

*F*ruit salad is not a time-consuming sweet to prepare, especially if you use large fruits such as mango and pineapple which are quick to peel and slice. Don't try to use too many different fruits as this will increase the preparation time – three or four varieties are fine. Other 'quick' fruits are bananas, peaches, melon, strawberries and raspberries. If you are going to make and eat a fruit salad straight away, it is important to have a good dressing, as the flavours won't have long to develop.

SERVES 4

1 mango, peeled and chopped
8 fresh dates, stoned and chopped
1 small fresh pineapple, diced
2 teaspoons lime or lemon juice
Juice of 1 orange
1 tablespoon clear honey
2 teaspoons desiccated coconut

Mix the fruits together and put into a serving dish.

Mix the fruit juices with the honey (this may be easier if the honey is warmed first), then pour this over the salad. Mix in well and serve decorated with desiccated coconut.

MARMALADE APPLES

Baked apples are so easy to prepare and lend themselves to a vast number of different fillings, but assembling an assortment of ingredients can be a little fiddly. This recipe uses a little marmalade mixed with orange juice which is simply poured over sultanas, making it quick to prepare.

SERVES 4

4 large cooking apples
2 tablespoons sultanas

2 tablespoons marmalade
4 tablespoons orange juice
Butter for greasing the baking
  dish

Pre-heat the oven to gas mark 5, 375°F (190°C).

Prepare the apples by washing and coring them. Then make a slit in the skin around the centre. Divide the sultanas between the apples and pack them in well. Warm the marmalade and orange juice in a small pan, then pour over the apples.

Place the apples in a buttered dish and bake for 35 minutes, basting occasionally. Serve hot.

FRUIT AND TOFU CREAM

*L*ike the recipe on page 99, this demonstrates tofu's versatility in combining with different flavours. As a contrast to the smooth texture, stir in some chopped banana and top the dessert with a bought granola or crunchy cereal. This pudding does need to be eaten fairly soon after it is made, as the banana will discolour. Other fruits to try in this type of purée are fresh peaches, strawberries and cherries.

SERVES 4

10 oz (275 g) silken tofu
2 bananas

Juice of 1 orange
Honey to taste
3–4 tablespoons granola

Blend the tofu with one of the bananas and orange juice and sweeten with honey to taste. Slice the other banana finely and mix in. Spoon the mixture into glasses and cover thickly with granola.

Opposite: Spiced Fruit Compote (page 97); Apricot Whip (page 98); and Fruit Ambrosia (page 100)
Overleaf: Cornmeal Pizza (page 110)

LIVENING-UP
THE LEFTOVERS

*T*his chapter includes some useful recipes to help you use leftovers, or turn what might otherwise be a dull or insubstantial mixture into a meal. These include a crumble topping, certainly the speediest of the choices, a savoury cornmeal batter and a basic pancake recipe. Use these ideas with your favourite casserole, stew or stir-fry mixture.

I've also included an all-in-one white sauce recipe which can be served with vegetables and topped with cheese for a quick supper, as well as a scone-based pizza, which is always popular and easy to make and lends itself to many variations.

There are some tips to help you save time by preparing things in advance. The trump card is ACE – Always Cook Extra – especially pulses, grains or any type of mixture that is suitable as a filling or stuffing.

Other items to keep in stock are some ready-made mixes for real emergencies. It is worth trying a few varieties to find your favourite. There is a good choice now of burger and croquette mixtures, pasta sauces and partially cooked grain mixes for pilaff and risotto.

QUICK TIPS

* Cook extra pulses or grains as they will keep in the refrigerator for 3–4 days. Use them in salads, casseroles and savoury fillings.
* Have some varieties of grains and pulses in the freezer. They will keep at least 6 months.
* Make soups and stews in large quantities as these freeze well and can be easily defrosted.
* Left-over stews can be transformed into new meals with a variety of toppings.
* For quick crumble topping, use a well-flavoured oil instead of rubbing-in a solid fat.
* Nuts and seeds add interest to a topping, either mixed in or sprinkled on top.
* Make pancakes in batches for the freezer. They do not need to be separated with pieces of greaseproof paper.
* Keep tomato sauce and pizza toppings in the freezer.
* Make extra breadcrumbs for nut burgers and similar dishes. Keep them in the freezer.
* Remember that many dishes improve in flavour if they are made in advance and reheated.

SAVOURY CORNMEAL TOPPING FOR VEGETABLES

*T*his is a very quick and tasty batter topping that can be used to cover most mixtures of vegetables. Remember to make the vegetable base quite moist so that it complements the sponge-like topping. When making the topping, don't forget that the amount of liquid you need may vary according to the type of flours you use and how long you have had them. Simply add more liquid gradually until the mixture reaches a pouring consistency. Once made, the batter should be cooked immediately.

4 oz (125 g) wholemeal self-
  raising flour
2 oz (50 g) fine cornmeal
Pinch salt

2 eggs
3 oz (75 g) butter or margarine
5 fl oz (150 ml) milk
1 tablespoon sunflower seeds

Pre-heat the oven to gas mark 6, 400°F (200°C).

Mix the flours and salt together. Using a food processor or blender, blend in the eggs and fat, then add enough milk to make a thick batter-type dough. Spoon the batter over any prepared vegetable mixture and sprinkle with sunflower seeds, then bake for 20–25 minutes.

CRUMBLE TOPPING

A crumble topping is one of the easiest ways to transform a mixture, sweet or savoury, into a presentable meal. To save time I use oil instead of a solid fat so there's no rubbing in. You'll find the crumble has a very crisp texture using this method. There are plenty of ways to vary the basic mixture. Use different flakes, oils or add a handful of nuts and seeds. For sweet crumbles, add dried fruit, honey or sugar and sweet spices.

2 oz (50 g) wholemeal flour
2 oz (50 g) porridge oats
1 oz (25 g) blanched almonds,
    chopped

2–3 tablespoons sunflower oil
Salt and black pepper

Pre-heat the oven to gas mark 5, 375°F (190°C).
   Mix the flour, oats and almonds together, then mix in the oil until it is well distributed. Add a little seasoning. Sprinkle this mixture over the prepared filling and bake for 25–30 minutes. Serve hot.

ALL-IN-ONE SAUCE

*I*t is possible to make a quick sauce by blending all the ingredients in a blender or food processor. Use a finely milled flour for this, and give the sauce time to simmer or the flour will not be cooked.

10 fl oz (300ml) milk
2 tablespoons wholemeal flour

1½ oz (40 g) butter or
    margarine
Salt and black pepper

Put the ingredients in a blender and blend for 10–15 seconds. Pour the liquid into a saucepan and heat gently, stirring constantly. When the sauce reaches boiling point, reduce the heat and simmer for 2–3 minutes.

Variations:
* Stir in mustard, horseradish or paprika to flavour the sauce.
* Cook some diced mushrooms in a separate pan and add to the sauce once it is cooked.
* Add grated cheese to the cooked sauce.

BASIC WHOLEMEAL PANCAKE

*P*ancakes are a marvellous way to make all sorts of fillings into interesting meals. As they can be prepared well ahead of time, or made in batches and frozen, they should be a standard part of your 'Quick and Easy' repertoire.

MAKES 8–10

10 fl oz (300 ml) milk
1 egg

1 teaspoon oil
4 oz (125 g) wholemeal flour
Pinch salt
A little oil for frying

Using a food processor or blender, mix the milk, egg and oil together for 30 seconds. Then add the flour and salt and blend again until smooth.

Using a small, preferably non-stick pan, heat a little oil and when the pan is smoking, add 2 tablespoons batter and fry the pancake for 2–3 minutes on either side.

If you are using them straight away, pile them up and keep them warm in the oven. If you wish to freeze them, leave them to cool, then stack in convient numbers and wrap well in greaseproof paper and foil. Separate them with pieces of greaseproof if you are likely to need only one or two. The stacks of pancakes will defrost in a couple of hours.

Pancakes can also be frozen filled as long as the filling is suitable for freezing.

To reheat pancakes: if they are not covered with a sauce, then they must be put in a greased dish and brushed with melted butter to prevent them drying out. Put them in a moderate oven for 20–25 minutes or in the microwave for 10 minutes.

CORNMEAL PIZZA

*T*his is a useful quick base to make for a pizza-style topping. The cornmeal adds a good flavour and appetising colour. There are plenty of variations possible for the topping. Add extra vegetables such as mushrooms or peppers, different herbs, olives or seeds.

SERVES 3–4

For the base:
4 oz (125 g) cornmeal
4 oz (125 g) wholemeal flour
1 teaspoon baking powder
¼ teaspoon salt
1 egg
5–6 fl oz (150–175 ml) milk
1 tablespoon olive oil

For the topping:
1 tablespoon olive oil
1 onion, peeled and finely
   chopped
1 clove garlic, crushed
1–2 tablespoons tomato purée
1–2 teaspoons dried oregano
4 oz (125 g) mozzarella cheese

Pre-heat the oven to gas mark 6, 400°F (200°C).

To make the base, mix the cornmeal, flour, baking powder and salt in a large bowl. In a jug beat the egg with the milk and olive oil. Gradually add this liquid to the dry ingredients to make a soft dough. If necessary add a little more milk. Press the dough onto a well-greased baking tray. Bake for 10 minutes.

Meanwhile make the topping. Heat the oil and gently fry the onion and garlic for 5–10 minutes or until quite soft. Then mix in the tomato purée, herbs and enough water to moisten the sauce. Season to taste. Spread the sauce over the pizza base. Then top with mozzarella cheese. Grill for 5–6 minutes to melt the cheese and serve straight away.

MEALS IN MINUTES!

*H*ere are six menus that include a wide variety of ideas for different types of meals: lunches, suppers, cold and hot. The one thing they all have in common is that they can be prepared, cooked and ready to serve in 30 minutes! The meals are simple and, of course, you can add to them as you wish depending on the time you have available. You'll find the recipes draw on some of the time-saving techniques that I've covered in the other chapters: there is, for example, a menu that includes stir-frying, one that uses the microwave, one that includes raw food, and one with quick-cooking basic ingredients. Each menu also has a time plan which sets out the order of work in 5-minute blocks. Once you have got used to this method of working, I think you'll find it will help you organise other menus and see what else can be achieved in a limited space of time.

To be successful, remember the following things.
* Clear the decks before you start so you have a good space for working.
* Assemble the ingredients you need or at least have them close to hand.
* Read through the plan and the recipes which follow before you start.

Good luck!

SUMMER SALAD

*S*alads certainly needn't be insubstantial meals, nor do they only contain greenery. This menu consists of an unusual Marinated Mushroom and Walnut Salad, a simple fresh coleslaw, and baked potato. There is a delicious peach and ginger dessert to follow. The menu is a slight cheat in that it relies on using a microwave – especially for the potatoes. However, these and the other dishes can be cooked conventionally.

SERVES 4

Marinated Mushroom and Walnut Salad
Carrot Coleslaw
Cheese and Herb Potatoes
Peaches with Ginger Yoghurt

Time Plan
30 mins: Make up the marinade for the mushroom and walnut salad, and add the mushrooms and spring onions. Microwave for 2 minutes.

25 mins: Scrub the potatoes and pierce. Put in the microwave and cook for 20–25 minutes.

20 mins: Make the coleslaw.

15 mins: Mix together the ingredients for the potato filling. Rearrange the potatoes in the microwave.

10 mins: Slice the peaches and set them in a micro-proof dish.
         Chop the ginger and mix with the yoghurt.

5 mins: Cut the potatoes open, mix the flesh with the cheese and herbs, pile the mixture back into the potatoes and reheat in the microwave.
         Add the walnut pieces and cherry tomatoes to the mushroom marinade and mix well.

To serve:
Put the two salads on the table and serve the potatoes separately. Whilst eating the first course, microwave the peaches for 2–3 minutes. Then serve them warm covered with the ginger-flavoured yoghurt.

MARINATED MUSHROOM AND WALNUT SALAD

*M*ushrooms are a wonderfully absorbent ingredient. They cook very quickly in a microwave and then can be left to stand for a short while to soak up the flavours of the pungent marinade. If I have any of this salad left over, I stir it into cooked rice and either have it cold or reheat it briefly in the microwave for a simple supper.

For the marinade:
2 fl oz (50 ml) olive oil
1 tablespoon white wine
   vinegar
1 tablespoon fresh basil,
   chopped
2 teaspoons prepared French
   mustard
1/2 teaspoon paprika

Salt and black pepper

12 oz (350 g) mushrooms,
   wiped and sliced
1 bunch spring onions, trimmed
   and chopped
6 oz (175 g) walnut pieces
8 oz (225 g) cherry tomatoes
1 flat lettuce

Make up the marinade by shaking all the ingredients together thoroughly in a screw-top jar. Season to taste.

Prepare the mushrooms and spring onions and mix into the marinade. Microwave for 2 minutes in a covered dish, then leave for 10–15 minutes.

Add the walnuts and tomatoes and mix in well. Line a serving bowl with salad leaves and pile the marinated mushroom mixture into the centre.

CARROT COLESLAW

*C*arrots add sweetness and moisture to any salad and they don't seem to lose this quality even when grated finely in a food processor. Cabbage is the traditional coleslaw ingredient, but I find Chinese leaves a more pleasant flavour. They do store well in the refrigerator if you need to buy them in advance.

2 medium carrots, peeled and grated
8 oz (225 g) Chinese leaves, finely shredded
2 tablespoons raisins or sultanas

1 tablespoon mayonnaise
Salt and black pepper
1 punnet salad cress

Mix the carrot and Chinese leaves with the raisins and mayonnaise. Season to taste. Serve garnished with salad cress.

CHEESE AND HERB POTATOES

4 × 8 oz (225 g) potatoes
2 oz (50 g) Cheddar cheese, grated
2 oz (50 g) cottage cheese
1 oz (25 g) butter

2 tablespoons fresh parsley, chopped
1 tablespoon chives or spring onions, chopped
Salt and pepper

Scrub the potatoes well and pierce well all over. Wrap in absorbent paper and arrange on a plate, evenly spaced. Cook in the microwave for 25 minutes. (Larger potatoes will take longer.) (This is the suggested time for 4 × 8 oz (225 g) potatoes and the time will vary according to the size.) Turn the potatoes over and re-arrange halfway through the cooking time. (If you are cooking them in a conventional oven, bake at gas mark 5, 375°F

(190°C) for 1½ hours.)

When the potatoes are virtually cooked, remove them from the microwave or oven and cut in half. Scoop out the flesh and mix it well with all the other ingredients. Season well. Pile the mixture back into the potatoes and reheat for 4 minutes in the microwave or for 10 minutes in the oven. Serve hot.

PEACHES WITH GINGER YOGHURT

*T*his is a simple dessert made more interesting by serving the peaches just warm and smothering them with a fresh ginger yoghurt.

4 ripe peaches   *1 oz (25 g) stem ginger,*
8 fl oz (250 ml) set yoghurt   *chopped finely*

Slice the peaches and stone them. Place in a dish suitable for the microwave. Cook for 2 minutes or until heated through.

Meanwhile, mix the yoghurt and chopped ginger together.

To serve the peaches, place them in separate bowls and smother with the yoghurt mixture.

STIR-FRY SUPPER

*T*his Oriental-style menu is very quick to cook once you have prepared all the vegetables. Served with noodles, it makes quite a substantial meal. The toasted nuts and seeds increase the protein level as well as adding texture. You could use tofu instead. I haven't included a starter, as the main point about stir-fries is that they should be eaten straight away.

SERVES 4

Toasted Cashew Stir-fry with Noodles
Creamy Cherry Dessert

Time Plan
30 mins: Assemble and prepare all the vegetables for the stir-fry.

20 mins: Put the cashews and sunflower seeds for the stir-fry in the micro-wave for 4 minutes or in the oven at gas mark 6, 400°F (200°C) for 5 minutes. Mix the sauce ingredients together.

15 mins: Add the shoyu to the nuts and toast again. Remove from the oven or microwave and put in a small bowl.

For the dessert, mix the jam with the cheese and double cream and spoon into small glasses.

Bring the water for the noodles to the boil.

10 mins: Begin the stir-fry.

5 mins: Put the noodles on to cook.

Complete the stir-fry and stir in the toasted nuts.

To serve: Drain the noodles and divide between four plates, heaping the stir-fry over the top.

TOASTED CASHEW STIR-FRY WITH NOODLES

*M*ixed nuts, seeds and beansprouts give this mainly vegetable dish a substantial amount of protein as well as contributing to the flavour and texture. With stir-fry mixtures, try to choose a colourful selection of vegetables and pick ones that work well when crisply cooked. I like to finish the dish off by cooking the mixture in the sauce but you could cook that separately, simmering it until it thickens and clears. Serve this stir-fry with quick-cooking noodles.

4 oz (125 g) cashew pieces
2 oz (50 g) sunflower seeds
2 teaspoons shoyu
2 teaspoons sunflower oil
1 clove garlic, crushed
8 oz (225 g) French beans, sliced
3 sticks celery, sliced
4 oz (125 g) mooli, diced
2 carrots, diced
8 oz (225 g) mushrooms, wiped and quartered
4 oz (125 g) beansprouts

For the sauce:
5 fl oz (150 ml) vegetable stock
1 tablespoon shoyu
Juice of ½ lemon
1 clove garlic, crushed
1 tablespoon concentrated apple juice
1 teaspoon Chinese 5 Spice
½ teaspoon arrowroot

8 oz (225 g) wholemeal noodles

Mix the nuts and seeds together and toast for 4 minutes in a microwave or for 5–7 minutes in the oven at gas mark 6, 400°F (200°C). Check them occasionally to prevent the pieces burning. Mix in 2 teaspoons shoyu and then put back in the microwave for 30 seconds or the oven for 2 minutes. Then leave to cool.

Prepare all the vegetables and have the oil and garlic to hand.

Mix the sauce ingredients together.

In a wok or large frying pan, heat the oil and add the garlic, beans, celery, mooli and carrots. Cook briskly for 3–4 minutes, stirring continuously. Add the mushrooms and beansprouts and cook for another 2 minutes, stirring all the time. Then pour over the sauce, stir in well and simmer for 3–4 minutes until the sauce thickens and coats the vegetables.

Mix in the toasted nuts and seeds and serve straight away.

   To cook the noodles, bring a large pan of salted water to the boil then add the noodles and cook for 4 minutes or until just tender. Drain well and serve immediately.

CREAMY CHERRY DESSERT

Sugar-free jams are great to use in quick puddings as they are full of fruit which blends easily into cream, soft cheese or yoghurt. You do need to use several spoonfuls to get a good flavour.

6–8 tablespoons sugar-free cherry jam

7 oz (200 g) quark or crème fraîche
2 fl oz (50 ml) double cream

Mix the jam thoroughly with the quark and double cream, then spoon the mixture into 4 small bowls or glasses.

Variation
Put a tablespoon of Morello cherries in each glass before topping it with the cherry cream.

SPRING LUNCH

*T*his is a quick and colourful light lunch that reminds me of spring but could easily be served at any time of the year. If you wish the meal to be more substantial, have some good wholemeal bread and butter on hand. If you want to prepare something in advance, the Hunza apricots can easily be cooked the day before and reheated or served cold.

SERVES 4

Cheese and Leek Ramekins
Hot Herby Mushrooms
Grilled Tomatoes
Poached Hunza Apricots

Time Plan
30 mins: Set the oven at gas mark 6, 400°F (200°C).
          Mix the Hunza apricots with the spice. Bring to the boil.
          Start to cook the leeks and garlic for the ramekins.

25 mins: Turn the apricots to simmer.
          Prepare the mushrooms and halve the tomatoes.

20 mins: Prepare the remaining ingredients for the Cheese and Leek Ramekins.
          Grease and line the ramekin dishes.

15 mins: Complete the ramekins and place in oven.
          Toast the almond flakes.

10 mins: Start to cook the mushrooms and mix dressing.
          Mix together the yoghurt and honey for the sauce to serve with the apricots.
          Grill the tomatoes.

5 mins: Remove the almonds from the oven.
          Toss the mushrooms in the dressing.
          Garnish the tomatoes.

To serve: Turn out the ramekins and portion out a helping of mushrooms and tomatoes on each plate. Garnish with parsley.

CHEESE AND LEEK RAMEKINS

*T*his is a tasty individual dish that works well as part of a light meal. Do chop the leeks finely (better still, use a food processor), or you will find they won't cook in the time.

1 tablespoon sunflower oil
1 lb (450 g) leeks, finely
  chopped
1 clove garlic, crushed
4 eggs, beaten

2 oz (50 g) breadcrumbs
4 oz (125 g) cheese, grated
1 tablespoon parsley, chopped
Salt and black pepper

Pre-heat the oven to gas mark 6, 400°F (200°C).

Heat the oil and cook the leeks and garlic for 10 minutes.

In a separate bowl, mix together the eggs, breadcrumbs, cheese and parsley. Add the cooked leeks and mix in thoroughly. Season to taste.

Grease and line four ramekin dishes. Spoon in the mixture and bake for 15 minutes. Turn out and serve.

HOT HERBY MUSHROOMS

*H*ot mushrooms make a good moist accompaniment to a dry dish when you haven't time to make a sauce.

1 oz (25 g) butter or margarine
1 lb (450 g) button mushrooms,
  wiped
1 clove garlic, crushed
Juice of ½ lemon

1 teaspoon lemon rind
1 teaspoon clear honey
1 teaspoon prepared mustard
1 teaspoon dried marjoram
Salt and black pepper

Gently melt the butter and cook the mushrooms with the garlic for 5 minutes.

Mix the remaining ingredients together. Pour the dressing into the pan. Stir in well. Season to taste. Serve warm.

GRILLED TOMATOES

*T*hese are no trouble to prepare and add a colour and fresh flavour to the meal.

8 tomatoes	*Sprigs of watercress*
A little olive oil	*Salt and black pepper*

Slice the tomatoes in half and brush with olive oil. Grill for 5–7 minutes. Garnish with watercress. Season to taste.

POACHED HUNZA APRICOTS

*T*hese are a delicious fruit with a mild flavour. Although they are dried, they reconstitute very quickly – the main thing to remember is to cover them with plenty of water. To make the pudding a little more special, serve it decorated with toasted almonds.

12 oz (350 g) Hunza apricots	For the sauce:
1 stick cinnamon or 6 allspice	*1 × 7 oz (200 g) carton Greek*
berries	*yoghurt*
2 tablespoons flaked almonds	*2 teaspoons clear honey*

Wash the apricots and cover them with plenty of water. Bring to the boil with the spice and then cover the pan and simmer for 30–40 minutes. Remove the spices.

Toast the almonds at gas mark 6, 400°F (200°C) for 7 minutes.

Mix together the ingredients for the sauce.

Serve the apricots in individual bowls decorated with almonds and hand the sauce separately.

MEZZE

SERVES 4

Humus	*Olives*
Tzatziki	*Marinated Chillies*
Pitta Bread	*Ricotta and Honey Pudding*
Simple Mixed Salad	

This menu is deliberately based around shop-bought items, leaving you the minimum to do to make a meal. The food is served buffet style, with everything on the table at once, making a most attractive feast. Obviously if you have more time you can add home-made dishes such as Bulgar Wheat Bake (page 31) or Persian Pilaff (page 30).

Time Plan

30 mins: Peel and grate the cucumbers for the Tzatziki. Salt lightly and leave in a bowl under a weight.

Make the Humus and leave it to stand for the flavour to develop.

25 mins: Toast the chopped nuts for the Ricotta and Honey Pudding under the grill for 2–3 minutes or in the microwave for 1 minute.

Make the pudding, beating the ricotta with the brandy, honey, cream and cinnamon. Spoon into small ramekins and chill.

20 mins: Assemble the mixed salad ingredients and toss together in a large bowl. In a separate jar, mix the dressing together.

15 mins: Drain and rinse the cucumbers and mix with the yoghurt, garlic and mint. Put it into a serving dish and chill.

10 mins: Put the olives and chillies in serving dishes.

Check the Humus and adjust the seasonings if necessary, then put it into an attractive serving dish. Heat the pitta bread.

5 mins: Toss the salad and dressing.

Garnish the Humus with lemon slices, and the Tzatziki with mint leaves.

Decorate the pudding with chopped nuts.

To serve:

Put all the bowls on the table. Leave the pudding in the refrigerator until needed.

HUMUS

*H*umus is a classic Greek dish made with chick peas, tahini, lemon juice and garlic. It is ideal to make with tinned chick peas, as they are generally fairly soft and easier to grind to a smooth consistency. This version is enriched with olive oil, which gives the dish a marvellous velvet texture.

1 × 14 oz (400 g) tin of chick
*   peas*
Juice of ½ lemon
1–2 cloves garlic, crushed
1 tablespoon olive oil
2–3 tablespoons tahini

2–3 tablespoons vegetable
*   stock*
Salt and black pepper

Lemon slices to garnish

Drain the chick peas and put in a blender or food processor with the lemon juice, garlic and oil. Blend well. It is best to use short bursts and then scrape the mixture from around the sides using a spatula. Add the tahini and stock and blend again until very smooth and thick. If you wish to thin the mixture add more stock. If it is too runny add more tahini. Let the humus stand for a while, then taste and add more lemon juice and seasoning to taste. Garnish with slices of lemon. Serve with bread or crackers.

TZATZIKI

*T*his is a classic Middle Eastern dish made with grated or puréed cucumber and yoghurt, well spiked with garlic. If you can, use the Greek or Cypriot cucumbers, as they are firmer and have a stronger flavour.

*2 Greek or Cypriot cucumbers or
    ½ standard cucumber
A little salt
4 tablespoons natural yoghurt*

*1 clove garlic, crushed
1–2 tablespoons fresh mint,
    chopped
Pepper*

Peel the cucumber and grate finely. Put the pulp in a bowl and sprinkle lightly with salt, then cover with a weighted plate. Leave for 10 minutes or so, then rinse and drain well.

Mix the cucumber with the yoghurt, garlic and mint. Season to taste. Serve chilled.

SIMPLE MIXED SALAD

*T*his is a simple mixed salad that goes well with the rest of the meal. You can always extend it by adding other leaves, particularly radicchio or endive or different coloured peppers. If you know all your guests like olives, these can be mixed in as well.

*1 Cos lettuce or other crisp-
    leafed variety
8 oz (225 g) firm tomatoes
1 bunch spring onions, trimmed
    and chopped
1 green pepper, de-seeded and
    diced*

For the dressing:
*2 tablespoons olive oil
Juice of ½ lemon
1 clove garlic, crushed
½ teaspoon dried rosemary
½ teaspoon dried oregano
Salt and black pepper*

Prepare the vegetables for the salad and mix in a large bowl.
Mix the dressing ingredients together and season to taste.
Just before serving, toss the salad into the dressing.

RICOTTA AND HONEY PUDDING

*T*his very simple pudding is quick to make and so rich that you need only serve it in small portions. When soft fruits are available in the summer months, you could easily use this mixture as a topping over sliced peaches, nectarines or cherries. Change the spirit to suit the fruit!

8 oz (225 g) ricotta cheese
4 teaspoons honey
4 teaspoons brandy or liqueur
2 tablespoons double cream
1 teaspoon ground cinnamon

For the decoration:
1 tablespoon chopped nuts

Beat the ricotta with all the other ingredients until quite smooth then pile into small dishes.

Toast the nuts in the microwave for 1 minute or under the grill for 2–3 minutes, shaking frequently to prevent the pieces burning.

Sprinkle a few nuts on each dessert just before serving.

WINTER SUPPER

SERVES 4

Poached Pears with Raspberry Vinaigrette
Chilli Bean and Mushroom Casserole with Rice
Broccoli with Lemon Butter and Almonds
Cheese Board

A richly flavoured stew is welcome on cold evenings and doesn't take too long to prepare. Cook this chilli in a pressure cooker so that it is ready in the time allowed, and serve with brown rice, a steamed green vegetable and sour cream for a splendid main course. The poached pear starter is a refreshing combination of flavours and, to keep the menu simple, I suggest you finish with cheese and biscuits. If you had more time a fruit crumble or microwaved steamed pudding would complement the chilli.

Time Plan
30 mins: Boil some water for the rice. Measure and begin to cook the rice.
Prepare the onion and garlic for the chilli, and begin to cook.

25 mins: Prepare the vegetables for the chilli, assemble the spices and drain the tin of beans.

20 mins: Add the vegetables, beans and spices to the onion and garlic and stir well. Purée the tomatoes and add them to the pan with the remaining ingredients.

15 mins: Bring the chilli to pressure and cook for 15 minutes.
Prepare the pears.

10 mins: Prepare the broccoli.
Poach the pears.
Arrange the cheese board.
Check the rice.

5 mins: Steam or microwave the broccoli.
Mix the poached pear dressing. Set out and garnish the pears.

To serve: Depressurise the chilli, then return the pan to a low heat. Put cooked rice in the oven to keep warm whilst eating the first course.

POACHED PEARS WITH RASPBERRY VINAIGRETTE

*T*his is an unusual starter with a refreshing taste.

2 large pears, peeled and thinly sliced
10 fl oz (300 ml) orange juice
2 tablespoons sunflower oil

1 tablespoon raspberry vinegar
1 tablespoon honey
Grated nutmeg

Prepare the pears and poach the slices in the orange juice for 5 minutes.

Mix the oil, vinegar and honey with 4 tablespoons of the poaching liquid.

Put the pear slices on 4 small plates and pour over a little dressing. Garnish with a little grated nutmeg. Serve warm.

CHILLI BEAN AND MUSHROOM CASSEROLE

1 tablespoon olive oil
1 onion, peeled and finely chopped
1 clove garlic, crushed
1 red pepper, de-seeded and diced
8 oz (225 g) mushrooms, wiped and halved
½ teaspoon chilli powder
½ teaspoon ground cumin
1 teaspoon dried thyme

1 × 14 oz (400 g) tin of tomatoes, puréed
1 × 14 oz (400 g) tin of red kidney beans
1 tablespoon tomato purée
1 tablespoon shoyu
5 fl oz (150 ml) vegetable stock
Salt and black pepper

To serve:
5 fl oz (150 ml) sour cream

Heat the oil and gently fry the onion for 3 minutes, then add the garlic, vegetables and spices and stir in well. Cook for 2 minutes. Add the remaining ingredients and bring the mixture to pressure. Cook for 15 minutes, depressurise and season to taste. Serve straight away, with the soured cream in a separate bowl.

BROCCOLI WITH LEMON BUTTER AND ALMONDS

1¼–1½ lb (550–700 g) broccoli,
   cut into florets
1 oz (25 g) whole almonds,
   coarsely chopped
1 oz (25 g) butter

1–2 teaspoons lemon juice
Black pepper
1 tablespoon fresh parsley,
   chopped

Steam the broccoli for 6–8 minutes or microwave in a covered dish with a little water for 7–8 minutes.

Toast the chopped almonds in the oven at gas mark 6, 400°F (200°C) for 7–10 minutes, or microwave for 2 minutes.

Melt the butter with the lemon juice in a separate pan. Season with black pepper.

Pour the melted butter over the freshly cooked broccoli and toss in the parsley and toasted almonds.

CHEESE BOARD

Choose three or four contrasting cheeses weighing 2–3 oz (50–75 g) each: a good mature Cheddar, a soft cheese such as Brie, a goat's cheese and a blue cheese such as Danish or Stilton. Decorate the board with celery, small apples, and black and green grapes. Serve with oatcakes or crackers.

ITALIAN DINNER

*T*his is an extremely easy menu. I've included my own recipe for olive pesto, but you could use a ready-made pesto sauce instead. (You should be able to buy this in a large supermarket; and if you live close to a good delicatessen, you may find they make their own.) Pesto will keep several weeks, as will dried pasta, so it is an ideal combination to have in the store cupboard.

SERVES 4

Avocado with Tomato and Orange
Pasta with Olive Pesto
Mushroom and Red Pepper Sauté
Plum and Raisin Crunch

Time Plan
30 mins: Wash and halve the plums and stew with the raisins and honey in orange juice for 10 minutes.
Prepare the dressing for the avocados.

25 mins: Prepare the avocado starter. Slice the oranges and tomatoes and dice the avocado. Toss the avocado in the dressing, then arrange the ingredients on plates and chill.

15 mins: Prepare the pepper and mushrooms for the sauté.
Spoon the plums into a serving dish, sprinkle with granola and keep warm.
Boil water for the pasta.

10 mins: Cook the mushroom sauté.

5 mins: Put the pasta on to boil.

To serve:
Serve the starter and leave the pasta to finish cooking. Just before serving the pasta, toss in the pesto sauce.

AVOCADO WITH TOMATO AND ORANGE

*T*his is a simple, colourful dish which makes a very attractive starter. Tossing the avocado in the dressing prevents it from going brown, so you can prepare it in advance.

1 large or 2 medium avocados
2 oranges
4 tomatoes

For the garnish:
Watercress sprigs

For the dressing:
2 tablespoons orange juice
1 tablespoon olive oil
1 teaspoon wine vinegar
Pinch allspice
Salt and black pepper

Peel the avocado and chop into neat dice. Peel the oranges and slice into rings. Slice the tomatoes.

Mix the ingredients for the dressing together and season to taste.

Toss the avocado dice in the dressing.

Using small plates, lay alternate slices of tomato and orange across the middle. Then divide up the avocado between the four plates. Garnish with watercress sprigs.

PASTA WITH OLIVE PESTO

*I*t is worth having a jar of ready-made pesto in the store cupboard to use when you are very short of time. You can simply toss it into freshly cooked pasta or use it as a seasoning in sauces and casseroles. Pesto is a paste made from olive oil, basil, pine kernels and Parmesan cheese, but you can make many variations on this theme. I like adding olives to give a robust flavour.

1 lb (450 g) pasta, preferably
* tagliatelle*
A little olive oil
Salt

For the pesto:
3 oz (75 g) pitted black olives
1 oz (25 g) pitted green olives
2 oz (50 g) grated Parmesan
1 oz (25 g) fresh basil
1 tablespoon lemon juice
1 tablespoon capers
2 tablespoons olive oil
1 clove garlic

Purée the ingredients for the pesto in a blender or food processor to make a smooth taste. Adjust the quantities of olive oil or lemon juice if you prefer a sharper or smoother taste.

Bring a large pan of water to the boil. When it is boiling add the pasta, oil and salt. Cook the pasta for 8–10 minutes, testing toward the end of cooking – it is ready when the pieces still have a little bite to them. Drain well and immediately toss in the pesto sauce. Serve at once.

MUSHROOM AND RED PEPPER SAUTÉ

*T*his combination of vegetables makes a colourful side dish to complement the green of the pesto and pasta.

1 tablespoon olive oil
1 clove garlic, crushed
1 lb (450 g) mushrooms, wiped
  and chopped

1 red pepper, de-seeded and
  diced
1 teaspoon shoyu

Heat the oil and gently fry the garlic for 30 seconds. Add the mushrooms and pepper and mix well. Continue frying over a low heat for 5–7 minutes until quite soft. Add the shoyu and stir well. Serve immediately.

PLUM AND RAISIN CRUNCH

*R*aisins, orange juice and honey make a delicious sauce for the plums. Adding granola is the speediest way to make a mock crumble.

1 lb (450 g) dessert plums
10 fl oz (300 ml) orange juice
4 oz (125 g) raisins

1 tablespoon clear honey
3–4 tablespoons granola

For serving:
1/4 pint (150 ml) single cream

Wash and halve the plums and remove the stones. Put the pieces in a pan with the orange juice, raisins and honey. Bring the mixture to the boil and simmer, covered, for 10 minutes or until the fruit is fairly soft. Check for sweetness. Spoon the cooked fruit into a serving dish and sprinkle over the granola. Leave it in a warm place to soak in for 10 minutes or so. Serve warm with cream.

INDEX